P9-DNC-523

The WAR on MOMS

On Life in a Family-Unfriendly Nation

Sharon Lerner

John Wiley & Sons, Inc.

For my mother, Helen

Published by John Wiley & Sons, Inc., Hoboken, New Jersey
Published simultaneously in Canada

For general information about our other products and services, please contact our Customer Care Department within the United States at (800) 762-2974, outside the United States at (317) 572-3993 or fax (317) 572-4002.

Wiley also publishes its books in a variety of electronic formats. Some content that appears in print may not be available in electronic books. For more information about Wiley products, visit our web site at www.wiley.com.

Library of Congress Cataloging-in-Publication Data:

Lerner, Sharon, date.
The war on moms: on life in a family-unfriendly nation/Sharon Lerner.
p. cm.
Includes bibliographical references and index.
ISBN 978-0-470-17709-9 (cloth)
1. Working mothers—United States. 2. Stay-at-home mothers—United States. 3. Motherhood—United States. 4. Women—Employment re-entry—United States. 5. Choice (Psychology) I. Title.
HQ759.48.L49 2010
306.874'3—dc22 2009031384

Printed in the United States of America

10 9 8 7 6 5 4 3 2 1

Contents

Acknowledgments v

Introduction 1

1 Falling: When Needs Bring Families Down 6

2 Supermom Returns: Doing It All without Having It All 23

3 'Til Dishes Do Us Part: The Problem with Blaming Men 37

4 The Problems We Wish We Had: A Couple of Choices, None of Them Good 57

5 Testing the Bootstraps: What Exactly Is Keeping the Women of Mississippi Down? 76

6 Congratulations, Now Back to Work: Keeping Mothers and Babies Apart 93

7 Good Day Care Is Hard to Find: The Working Mom Crisis 121

8 The Elusive Part-Time Solution: The Stay-at-Home Mom Crisis 141

9 Baby Strike: The International Motherhood Experiment 160

10 The Blame Game: How and Why We Wound Up in Last Place 172

Epilogue 188

Notes 197

Index 211

Acknowledgments

The best part of writing this book has been the many great people who have shepherded it—and me—through the process. First and foremost, I owe my thanks to the dozens of women (and a few men) from across the country who took the time, trouble, and courage to speak to me about their lives. If they hadn't found ways to meet me on their breaks from work, call me at nap time, invite me into their homes and workplaces, and otherwise go to great lengths to fit me into their busy schedules, this book would not exist.

I am extremely grateful to my editor, Eric Nelson, who has remained committed to this book throughout its many incarnations and has drawn on his substantial creative powers to get the issues covered here read by a wide audience. Thanks also to my agent, Heather Schroder, and her crew at International Creative Management, who have shown great generosity to me and to this project.

I am indebted to all the people who made my research trips possible, providing everything from maps and meals to rides to the airport. Barbara Weinstein and Linda Carmona Sanchez gave me extraordinary guided tours of Florida child-care centers. Mary Westly, Susan Hill, and Betty Thompson were wonderfully trusting and helpful in Mississippi. Anmarie Widener shared her vast knowledge of the Netherlands. Nicolette and Flor Bunnik graciously welcomed my entire hungry and tired family into their Amsterdam home. Susan Loubet in New Mexico arranged important meetings as well as a family trip to the Albuquerque Zoo.

I also appreciate the many knowledgeable people who helped me find and understand the research I've reported on here, from the experts in the census bureau, who spent inordinate amounts of time on the phone explaining various statistics, to those who dug up data and crunched numbers at my request. Though I can't name everyone, I'd like to credit a few individuals: Matt Broaddus of the Center for Budget and Policy Priorities, Andrew White at the Center for New York City Affairs, Jocelyn Mazurkiewicz at the Labor-Management Project, Wendy Chavkin at the Columbia School of Public Health, David Cotter of Union College, Ron Rindfuss at the Carolina Population Center, Sophia Lee, and Malin Eberhard-Gran.

I am thankful to Francine Deutsch, Danielle Ewen, and Anmarie Widener for their comments on earlier drafts of this work; Jodi Levin-Epstein at the Center for Law and Social Policy for her guidance throughout the process, and to the Annie E. Casie Foundation for its support. The editing work of Betsy Reed and Alex Star helped shape the chapters on child care and the "international motherhood experiment," respectively. I also thank Jessica Dickson for her meticulous help with fact-checking and footnotes and Ellen Bilofsky for her careful reading.

I have been lucky to share an office with Holly Morris, who supplied me with much-needed lunch, heat, and encouragement throughout much of the writing process. My sister Marcia Lerner gave of her considerable editing expertise. Her read was thoughtful, meticulous, and astoundingly quick. I thank Karen Cook for her critical eye and for her friendship. Yuko Uchikawa lent her impeccable design sense and positive attitude. Toby Cox has been, as always, a trusty and supportive friend both on the road and at home. I am fortunate that countless others have also been tolerant and kind with me throughout this process, including Kate Milford, Rose Thomson, Nina Harris, and my sister Rachel Lerner.

I am especially grateful to all the child-care providers who made my work possible. My particular thanks to Angelica Roldos and her crew, whose home-based care was the most accommodating and loving I've ever encountered, and to the indefatigable Benjamin Schultz-Figueroa. Finally, I owe my deepest gratitude to my family. Life with Sam and Elijah offers daily humbling reminders of the reasons people still attempt to "do it all." Lucas Dreamer has been far more patient, caring, and accepting throughout the research and writing of this book than I ever imagined possible. He is a reader, listener, booster, father, and partner extraordinaire (and, for the record, a far neater person than I).

Introduction

With a sleeping baby strapped to her and a two-year-old loosely orbiting her knees, Angela could be the poster mom for carefree child-raising—at least from afar. As the summer sunlight angles down in the playground around them, Angela's older child laughs, seemingly at nothing other than the delight of treating her mother's legs like a maypole. From time to time, the baby briefly peeks out from his cocoon before pressing his face back into his mother's chest.

The only one in this idyllic tableau who doesn't seem content is Angela. From up close, it's clear her mind is elsewhere. Her fine features are arranged in a distracted grimace and she heaves a heavy sigh or two before she speaks. It's no wonder. With her maternity leave about to end, Angela just learned that she'll have to choose between working full-time and quitting. Although she had put in four-day weeks in the human resources department of a big bank for two years before her second child was born, her boss told her that this option was no longer available. Now, she would either have to be away from her children some fifty hours a week or give up her job entirely—along with the much-needed income and health insurance it provided her and her children.

Some choice!

Angela is not the only one facing such unviable "options." Perhaps you yourself work so hard, you don't have enough time for your family, let alone for yourself. On the other hand, you might have ample time with your children but feel edged out of professional life, unable to earn any money—or enough of it to avoid sinking into a financial hole. Or maybe you work hard and still find yourself barely getting by. Any of these scenarios is common. What's far less likely is that you have both financial stability and all of the time you need to care for your family. That's because such balance has become a rare privilege in this country. And while it's easy to feel personally responsible for failing to achieve the elusive mix of work and family within your own life, the problem is far bigger than you—or than Angela, whatever decision she makes.

To say there is a sinister plot against American women is both overblown and exactly right. Technically speaking, there is no War on Moms, of course. There is no concerted effort to kill or maim women who have children. But if some sinister think tank had spent the last thirty years cooking up the ideal way to make American women miserable, it likely couldn't have served up more unpleasantness than women now encounter on a daily basis.

Looking only at our nation's current employment figures, you might think the problem of gender inequity had been solved. As of this writing, women make up half of the paid workforce—the highest percentage in U.S. history. This statistic is, on its surface, the happy consequence of decades of striving. But the day-to-day struggles of women living this "dream" were surely not envisioned by past generations of women. Who marches on Washington so she can wind up in a thankless, low-paying job or two or even three jobs with no health benefits? Or, perhaps, end up having gratifying work that requires so much commitment, there's no time left for anything else? Or finish the day so stressed out from trying to support her family that there's no time left to actually spend with them?

The sad fact is that the simple presence of women in the paid workforce hasn't meant equal pay, significantly higher earnings, or anything close to an even gendered split of the real power in our country. Equality has most definitely not dawned. Instead, without much increased flexibility in work schedules, guaranteed paid maternity leaves (or, as we'll see, sometimes any maternity leave at all), and, most important, any significant alleviation of women's burdens outside the workplace, life in its overwhelming, multitasking reality has become increasingly hellish for women in this country. If no one is aiming actual projectiles at mothers, the willful refusal to acknowledge and address the conditions that make so many of their lives unmanageable amounts to a very real assault.

Metaphorical though it may be, this "war" (with apologies to soldiers everywhere) nevertheless involves real enemies and clever tactics. It's easy for mothers to feel as if our opponents are women who have chosen different paths than we have, or even to blame ourselves for our problems. But this contortion of the notion of choice masks a deep structural unfairness. Our true adversaries are not within ourselves or our ranks. They are the many forces in business and government that elevate profit and sometimes political ideology above human needs. The stunning ability to ignore the duress this system of priorities has caused in women's lives is just one of the warriors' brilliant tactics. Another is to lay the blame for the crippling system elsewhere.

Like a real military operation, the War on Moms also has devastating casualties. Women who attempt to do "it all" suffer in terms of exhaustion, physical and mental ailments, and time to care for themselves and others, including their children and elderly family members. Other women get nudged out of work, contributing to sky-high poverty rates among American women and children. Still other women put off having children, or forgo the experience altogether, because they fear the costs to their careers.

Yet, as much as this open hostility toward families shapes women's existence, lowering their overall quality of life and influencing almost every important decision they make, the war, as it were, is being waged on all parents, regardless of gender, and really on all caretakers, whether they're looking after children or sick or elderly relatives. Unless people have unusually sensitive, flexible, and generous employers, almost anyone with pressing responsibilities to other humans will run into the same problems at some point.

Given what we know now, we might want to go back in time and warn past generations to be careful what they wish for. *Psst! As it turns out, acceptance in the public sphere isn't all that it's cracked up to be.* But the lesson can't be that women shouldn't have attempted—and continue to attempt—to scale the walls of discrimination, to have both work and family. Rather, it's that part of the immense task of integrating ourselves into the public sphere is both valuing—and getting help within—what has traditionally been the private one. Convincing government and workplaces to take on more of this domestic burden will require nothing short of a massive cultural shift, but the shift is long overdue. The first step is recognizing our failure to more evenly spread the responsibilities thus far for what it is: a full-on attack on women and their families.

1

Falling
When Needs Bring Families Down

Some turning points announce themselves clearly. With the snap of a spine or the reading of a good-bye note, everything is suddenly transformed. Other crossroads register only after they've passed. Such was the case for Bob and Devorah Gartner. Their troubles mounted gradually and steadily until, at some moment—no one can remember when, exactly—they realized they no longer inhabited their former life. Somehow, their financial comfort—indeed, most comforts—had slipped away.

There was a time when the Gartners had money, not a lot, just enough so they rarely thought about it. Devorah likes to call it their "yuppie phase," an era that peaked around 2000. As Devorah tells it, the couple practically rode into the twenty-first century on a gilded chariot, or at least a roomy, newish sedan, of which Devorah and Bob then had two. They lived in a co-op they owned in a wealthy Long Island suburb of New York City. Both worked full-time: Bob managed the library of a major law firm, and Devorah maintained computer software for another big firm. The two had a combined income of more than $100,000 and substantial retirement accounts, took regular vacations, bought clothes when they wanted them, and frequently indulged their appetite for nouvelle cuisine.

Almost nine years later, Devorah can recall the details of her former life as if it were yesterday. A voluble woman with a quick wit, straight light-brown hair, and a velvety voice, she squints into the middle distance as she works to remember, as if she could actually see back in time to the pleasant rhythm of their lives, the occasional nights spent out in a jazz bar or lingering over trout almondine and good wine in one of their favorite restaurants. Sitting beside her, Bob, a stocky man with a heavy beard and glasses, nods at the memory. "We were comfortable," he says. They agree, too, that whenever the exact moment their downward slide began, it was sometime after they got the best of news.

Having survived ovarian cancer when she was twenty-three and then cervical cancer thirteen years later, Devorah had virtually no chance of getting pregnant. One of her ovaries had been removed with the first cancer, and afterward she had undergone both chemotherapy and radiation, all of which had reduced her chances of conceiving. The only reason her doctors had held off performing a radical hysterectomy when they removed her tumors was that they feared she was too frail to withstand the operation. Yet at thirty-seven, while she and Bob were exploring the adoption process and trying to make peace with infertility, Devorah was astounded to discover that she was somehow pregnant.

She didn't tell Bob the news at first because she couldn't believe it herself. Even after a late period, several positive home tests, and a visit with her doctor, during which he reassured her several times that she was indeed pregnant, it took a while for the fact to sink in. Once it did, Devorah was overwhelmed with the immediate need to tell Bob in person, and she bounded giddily out of their Long Island apartment, onto the commuter train to New York City, and into Bob's office—wearing two different shoes. Bob was similarly overjoyed.

But the Gartners' elation was soon tempered by the sobering knowledge that as a two-time cancer survivor, Devorah could have serious problems carrying a healthy baby to term. As they feared, the pregnancy was difficult almost from the beginning. Devorah had asthma as a result of her cancer treatment, and, within weeks of her trip to the city in mismatched shoes, the condition severely worsened. One night, in the middle of a severe hurricane, she had a major attack. As the rain hammered down outside her window, Devorah, who was then four months along, desperately struggled to breathe. Her asthma meds gave little relief, and her wheezing and gasping were soon accompanied by spotting. Although such bleeding can sometimes signal the beginning of a miscarriage, her obstetrician suggested that Devorah wait out the storm before going to the hospital.

She spent that night fighting for breath and fretting over the fate of her pregnancy. When the morning finally dawned and Devorah made her way through the flooded roads to the hospital, she rejoiced in the pulsing light on the ultrasound monitor. Somehow, the tiny being within her had survived the night. Her doctor was still worried, though, and from that point on insisted on weekly sonograms. The tests revealed unsettlingly slow fetal growth, and eventually Devorah was put on bed rest, forbidden to get up even to go to the bathroom.

Devorah followed her doctor's orders, lying still in bed for months, but the baby came early anyway, six weeks before her due date. In the first few moments after Bethanie emerged into the world, tiny and, as is typical for premature babies, without eyebrows or eyelashes, she seemed miraculously free of serious health problems. But within twenty minutes, as Devorah was still counting and recounting her daughter's fingers and toes, Bethanie suffered a dramatic loss of blood pressure and stopped breathing. The doctors realized that she had a hole in her heart and rushed her to surgery.

Bethanie survived the operation, but the two weeks afterward, which her parents spent almost entirely in the neonatal intensive care unit, were an emotional roller coaster. Devorah and Bob watched helplessly as their small, frail daughter seemed to be improving one day, only to suffer a major setback the next. She struggled just to maintain her temperature, nurse, and breathe. Because she was skinny, Bethanie's eyes appeared far too big for her face. The incubator, with its mess of wires, tubes, and beeping devices, made her look even smaller.

When Bethanie began to stabilize, Bob and Devorah experienced a disorienting mix of emotions. First and foremost, there was profound relief that their daughter finally seemed to be on the road to survival. They felt as if they could breathe freely for the first time in weeks. But once they let their singular focus on Bethanie's well-being soften, anxiety about their mounting medical bills began to creep in. Because the health insurance Devorah had through Bob's job didn't cover weekly sonograms (and coverage through her own job hadn't kicked in yet), the couple had already put more than $200 a week on their credit cards for the prenatal tests. Now, on top of that debt were the hospital costs. Having exceeded the $80,000 cap on their major medical insurance, they owed $23,000 in medical bills even before leaving the hospital, most of which was the cost of intensive care for tiny Bethanie.

Out of cash and having maxed out their credit cards, they covered some bills with bad checks. Others they simply ignored. Unable to keep up with their monthly mortgage payments, they decided that they had no choice but to sell their apartment when Bethanie was only two months old. Partly because of their urgent need for cash, they did so quickly, at a considerable loss.

With medical debt rapidly swallowing up their income and savings, the Gartners were badly in need of a stroke of good luck. It came from a synagogue in upstate New York, where Devorah had volunteered on weekends for almost ten years. The congregation owned a house that had recently become vacant, and, after hearing the Gartners' saga, the temple's director offered a temporary solution: the family could stay in the house rent free if, in exchange, Devorah would teach religious school. The welcome act of generosity might have allowed the family to pull out of their financial crisis, if not for a new crop of medical problems that arose just as they began to settle into their new home.

Bethanie was just eight months old at the time and already behind the developmental curve. Up until this point, although she had yet to sit up or even roll over, her parents and doctors had attributed the delays to prematurity. Babies born before their due dates often lag in terms of walking, talking, and the precursors to those milestones. But more than half a year after Bethanie was born, as she should have been learning to crawl, it became apparent that she was developing motor skills even later than most preemies did. She was trying, that much was clear. But even when she scrunched up her face with the effort of attempting to get around, only her left side moved and she managed a strange sideways slither.

The sideways motion was what ultimately led Bethanie's doctors to deduce that the baby was partially paralyzed, most likely as a result of a stroke she had experienced in the uterus during Gartner's severe asthma attack. Her diagnosis—a lesion in the motor-planning area of her brain—helped explain the slither, as well as difficulties she had in learning to swallow, reach for things, and crawl. It also meant that she would need immediate long-term intensive therapy. Even then, there was no guarantee that she'd reach the physical milestones easily attained by most other children.

At this point, both Devorah and Bob were back at work full-time, trying to chip away at the family's debt. Bob worked the day shift, while Devorah, who had previously worked as a consultant to the firm that now directly employed her, spent her nights updating the company's word-processing software. She went into the office at eleven o'clock at night and emerged at seven the next morning, as the first rays of sun were hitting midtown Manhattan. The couple would meet at Grand Central Station on the way to and from work so that one parent could hand the baby off to the other before a shift. The pace was so exhausting that Gartner often fell asleep both at her job and while she was taking care of the baby. "If I slept two or three hours at a stretch those days, I was lucky," she recalls. "I was dozing off constantly, but I had to do things during the day, so I risked driving off the side of the road."

Between work and infant care, the Gartners didn't have a moment to spare. Yet after Bethanie's brain damage was confirmed, the doctors told them that the best hope for their daughter lay in frequent, intensive sessions of physical therapy. Six times a day, Bethanie was supposed to undergo a routine in which someone moved her arms and legs, brushed her body to stimulate her nerves, and massaged the inside and outside of her cheeks. This was on top of all the other things babies need: diaper changes and cuddling, naps and baths. Devorah still remembers the caretaking routine as "the hardest physical work I've done in my life."

As the consequences of Bethanie's stroke and the finite window of time they had to address them became more pronounced, Devorah realized that she had to take time off from work as soon as possible. She needed to consult with specialists, learn how to help and care for her baby, and train anyone else who would be looking after her. But she also needed and wanted to keep working. Despite the evening hours, she loved her job. She enjoyed the responsibility of keeping a large computer system humming. And the income was a crucial part of her plan to pull the family out of debt. Yet even though she earned $65,000 a year (almost twice what her husband made at the time), it would have taken years to pay off the more than $100,000 the family then owed.

Devorah hoped that she might take a month or so off to bring Bethanie's health crisis under control and then return to her assignment. So she sat down with the personnel director of her company, told her about her travails, and spelled out her request: she wanted six weeks off but would try to make do with three, if necessary. Devorah thought that she was being reasonable, accommodating even. But her higher-up flatly refused, noting that Devorah had already used up her sick and vacation time. As Devorah recalls, the woman said the firm simply couldn't "spare her."

What really stung was the personnel director's apparent annoyance with her request; Gartner remembers the woman calling it "inconvenient." A pet peeing on the rug is inconvenient. Having to reschedule a doctor's appointment is inconvenient. Uninvited houseguests can be inconvenient. But as both a mother and someone who had supported herself throughout her adult life up to this point, Devorah resented having that word applied to her situation. She was far beyond inconvenienced. She was desperate: frantic, exhausted, and always worried about money and her daughter. So, when her first request for time off was denied, she begged. After her second, groveling, and slightly teary plea for time off was rejected, Devorah took a deep breath and quit, knowing that she had no choice and that, without even unemployment coverage to tide her over, she was heading further into a terrifying financial hole.

There's nothing unusual about families teetering on and over the edge. The birth of a baby is one of the leading causes of poverty spells in the United States.[1] In addition, at last count, some 72 million people were struggling to pay their medical bills, so it's a rare family that wouldn't be destabilized by the combination of illness and infancy.[2] Indeed, Bob and Devorah Gartner can seem lucky—relatively, anyway. Unlike so many others, they at least had a roof over their head, health insurance, enough to eat, and each other to rely on. Their good fortune even extended to a caring community, their temple, which helped out when government, insurers, health-care providers, and employers did not.

Yet the family still wound up in the financial abyss as a direct consequence of basic needs. Despite being insured, educated, employed, and having a deep desire to be fiscally responsible, the Gartners simply couldn't stave off soaring debt. A difficult pregnancy and a sick baby were all it took to tear a family-size hole in the seemingly solid financial ground beneath them. Devorah had wanted so badly to have a baby, but now that she had one, it was as if the rest of her life was disintegrating. She felt under siege—and, in a way, she was.

People talk about work and life competing, but the truth is that life almost always wins. And, at least in terms of jobs and money, women almost always lose. Even the most obstinate personnel manager is no match for a sick baby. Although Devorah had had every intention of being a career mom and earned considerably more than her husband, she found herself edged out of the workplace. By way of explanation, she says first that Bob had better benefits and later that "Bethanie was very tiny and needed her mommy."

Once Devorah let go of her job, her descent began in earnest. Despite the fact that she had just joined the ranks of the unemployed, her days were full, with her time split between the tremendously consuming job of caring for her baby and the perhaps even more stressful task of financial triage. "If there was a choice between prescription drugs and groceries, we bought prescription drugs," says Gartner. "If there was a choice between groceries and the phone bill, we went without a phone." When she did have phone service, she spent hours on it, negotiating with utility companies and other creditors and pleading daily with her insurance company to cover disputed claims.

Despite her efforts, the process of becoming a have-not was fairly quick. Even living rent free, the Gartners were unable to cover many of their expenses, and their credit rating slipped from impeccable to below 500, the equivalent of a D. Although they liquidated their retirement accounts and borrowed from friends to help pay for essentials, there were several occasions on which Devorah found herself without enough cash for milk and diapers. Had she had the time to think about it as she was scrounging around for change under the couch in their temporary quarters, Gartner might have realized that her yuppie phase was officially over.

While Devorah Gartner was free falling, David Cotter was sitting in a cramped, hot office in Columbia, Missouri, surrounded by precarious stacks of paper and empty coffee cups. It was the summer of 2003, a hot one, and the sociologist was holed up in a drab cinder-block building, slogging through what was supposed to be a routine exercise. Cotter and two of his colleagues, Joan Hermsen and Reeve Vanneman, were sifting through huge national surveys to see how women were faring in the economy, politics, and public opinion. All three were used to the consistent advancement of women in these realms; indeed, much of their academic careers had been spent mapping women's continuous, mountainous ascent. But as they were plotting the most recent data points, they stumbled on what Cotter describes as the most important discovery of his career. For the first time in four decades, the lines weren't headed upward anymore. Everywhere they looked, what had not long ago been hopeful inclines were inexplicably leveling off or even pointing down.

You don't need a graph to know that the last half century has been defined by a rapid-fire series of achievements for women in almost every aspect of public life. Until very recently, these historic leaps forward have made parity with men seem inevitable. How could it end otherwise? The idea that women were biologically destined for less had given way under a mountain of milestones reached by female pioneers. When Cotter and crew were digging through their data, Oprah was already the top earner on television. Madeline Albright had already served as the first female secretary of state. A majority of college and medical school graduates were female. And countless women had muscled their way into the once gated professional communities of business, politics, and the military. It was no longer remarkable that women wrote and directed, choreographed and conducted, and, more and more, were viewed by both themselves and men as capable beings with relevant ideas. Equals.

Yet as Cotter's national data revealed, Devorah Gartner wasn't the only one losing her foothold. Women as a group appeared to be in the process of losing their momentum toward equality. Once virtually airborne, American women across racial, economic, and ethnic categories were apparently no longer catapulting forward. While many people already viewed the women's revolution as a mission accomplished or perhaps soon to be accomplished, the sociologists' numbers suggested otherwise. If their information was to be believed—and Cotter and his incredulous colleagues rechecked it several times—women were poised for a startling change.

Progress hadn't ceased all at once or even in the same way in various arenas of life. In some cases, women's giant steps forward had simply shrunk to small mincing ones. Women were still making inroads into traditionally male-dominated professions, for instance, but just much more slowly than they had been.[3] Ever since women have done paid work, they have always had different kinds of jobs than men had—most often, lower-paying ones. The huge numbers of women working in low-paid "pink collar" jobs as waitresses, secretaries, cashiers, elementary-school teachers, and child-care workers does a lot to explain the historic gender wage gap. For their part, men tend to be clumped in their own gender-specific lines of work, with some, such as airline pilot (98 percent male, according to the 2000 U.S. census), conferring considerable status, as well as relatively high salaries.[4] The country had been moving toward closing the occupational segregation gap over the last few decades. According to the best measure, occupational segregation dropped by about a fifth between 1960 and 1990.[5] Yet since then, movement toward integration had apparently ground to a near halt.

Women's advancement was also slowing in one of the most visible spheres: politics. The female presence in public office had by some measures continued to head back to earlier, lower levels. The number of women in the U.S. Congress has climbed steadily since 1950, when women made up 2 percent of the House of Representatives and zero percent of the Senate.[6] Yet as Cotter and his crew noted, the female presence in state legislatures, which had been dramatically growing since the 1970s, began to level off around 2000.[7] At the same time, the number of female state executives also headed south, dropping from around 28 percent in 2000 to 23 percent nine years later.[8]

Around the same time, progress on the wage gap had also come to a mysterious standstill of sorts. In 1963, women on average made 59 cents for every dollar earned by a man, a difference so appalling that feminists began to sport "59 cent" buttons.[9] That year, the Equal Pay Act was passed, which made it illegal for employers to pay men and women differently if they held the same jobs, and, partly as a result, the gender wage gap began to shrink. By 2001, the ratio of women's to men's median annual earnings for full-time, full-year workers was 76.[10] In other words, women made 76 cents for every dollar that men earned, still an inexcusable difference, but a vast improvement over a 41-cent one. Although that was clearly an improvement, the gap has stayed the same size for the last few years.

On closer inspection, it became clear that rather than simply closing, the pay gap was morphing in two big ways. First, the difference between men's and women's pay was getting smaller largely because men's wages were dropping, rather than women's rising.[11] And although the gap had gotten particularly small for women without children, who were finally earning almost as much as men who had a similar education, a new gap appeared to be opening. Once women had children, their earnings flattened or headed downward. Giving birth was the new financial turning point in many women's lives.[12]

In perhaps the most contentious and closely watched of all areas, participation in the workforce, women seemed to be moving backward. In 2000, 75 percent of women did paid work; by 2003, it had dropped to 72 percent.[13] While some challenged the idea that women overall were undergoing a shift, certain segments of women, especially mothers of young children, had clearly changed their work patterns. More married mothers of infants and preschool age children were staying out of the paid job market.[14]

Cotter mapped out the full, startling array of parallel trends in a 2006 paper he called "The End of the U.S. Gender Revolution." Depending on the version of the article, the title was sometimes followed by a question mark, at other times a period, and any fate—a nosedive, a leveling off, or a return to their previous ascent—still seems possible for American women.[15] Still, whether women are experiencing a major collective hiccup in their advancement or are headed for an inglorious mass landing, an important shift is clearly under way.

Indeed, recent changes in the forces affecting women don't bode well for a recovery. In the seven years since Cotter's discovery, most of which were stamped by a president who was unsupportive of, and sometimes hostile to, the needs and problems of everyday families, the already heavy pressures on women have clearly increased. A few of the hard-fought supports for American families came under attack as Lilly Ledbetter, who had challenged the fact that her male colleagues earned more than she did for the same work, found herself turned back by a court dominated by Bush appointees. The Bush administration made several Grinch-like attempts to restrict the already inadequate Family and Medical Leave Act.

Meanwhile, the crashing economy made conditions for everyone all the harder to bear. Since the downturn hit blue-collar jobs particularly hard, women's presence in the workforce has increased relative to that of men's.[16] But, like the apparent narrowing of the pay gap, this change still amounts to bad news for women, although perhaps slightly less bad than it has been for men. Because men and women alike are experiencing record high levels of unemployment, life is getting harder for everyone, including the increasing numbers of women who have become their family's sole breadwinner.

As child-care centers have gone out of business, families have lost their homes to foreclosure, and jobs have disappeared, countless women and families have come closer to their own boiling points. And the lines tracing women's achievements have yet to resume their upward climb.

Yet as profound as these documented shifts are, the slumping graph lines can't capture the epidemic of exhaustion sweeping through cubicles, cluttered kitchens, and child-care centers around our country. Call these women the maxed-out generation, if you like; victims of a family-unfriendly nation; or simply "hosed," as one friend likes to refer to herself when she can't work because her child care falls through. Allison Christian, a young mother of two in Birmingham, Alabama, decided on the term "zombymom" (definition: "females, usually sleep deprived, delirious, hormonal, without the ability to think, dazed, confused and absolutely worn out," according to her Web site, zombymom .com). Her entrepreneurial instinct told her that her fellow mothers would proudly wear the term emblazoned on their chests, and she started a company to make and sell the shirts. But, despite her business acumen and commitment to the idea, she found herself unable to juggle business and parenting responsibilities and ultimately abandoned the project.

There is now a great sea of beleaguered and overburdened people—mostly women, but, as I describe here, some men, too—stuck between the need to support their families and the desire to live decent lives with them. Single or part of a couple in which both partners work, they have no one at home to handle the inevitable overflow of domestic responsibilities, which leaves them impossibly squeezed by the combination of work and family that constitutes everyday life. I spoke to dozens of people like this in the three years I spent writing this book. It wasn't hard to find them: parents who couldn't afford child care or preschool; who stayed in dismal jobs for fear of losing their children's health insurance; who couldn't find those jobs with insurance in the first place; or who had to work so much to cover their families' expenses that they had no time to spend with them.

Who ultimately bears the responsibility for this immense sea of struggle? It's a question I explore through the stories of dozens of struggling parents like Devorah and Bob Gartner. In sorting through their experiences, along with the writings of policy makers and experts in the area, I've come to rethink some of our deeply rooted assumptions about the imbalance of work and life in this country. Thus, the first part of this book is devoted to exposing some of the most popular ideas as oversimplifications—and sometimes outright fictions. Perhaps the most insidious is that women are to blame for their problems, that they are overwhelmed and overworked simply because they've individually taken on too much or done a bad job coping with their responsibilities. Similarly unsatisfying is the theory that male partners alone are the root of the difficulties faced by women and families. Tackled last in this first section is the strangely persistent myth that all women share the struggles of professional women and that high-end employers might somehow be able to resolve them simply by tweaking their workplace policies. Clearly, each of these groups has some responsibility for the huge family-unfriendly mess we're in, although, as I show, not nearly as much as has been laid on them.

I then focus on what's really bringing American women down. Most often, these are things we lack, such as guaranteed paid maternity leave; decent, affordable child care;

health coverage; and good, flexible work options. These deficits function like sink holes or sand traps, into which women fall at critical junctures. In each case, there has been some awareness of the problem and some effort to fix it. But these solutions have been partial at best and, at worst, have dug American families further into a hole by giving them a false sense of "mission accomplished."

Lest these tales be taken as whining or the toll of child rearing be seen as inevitable, I take another chapter to look at how the United States compares internationally in terms of family-friendliness. I won't give anything away if I say now that we don't come off very well, and that most other rich countries show our difficulties to be quite real by escaping similar fates. Then I address how and why we fell so far behind as a nation and how we might get back. Finally, I attach a postscript that provides a last-minute update on the important changes, in both the government and the lives of the real people featured here, that have transpired while I've been writing this book.

2

Supermom Returns

Doing It All without Having It All

Who is responsible for women's collective and individual suffering? To the extent that anyone's asking, people often pin the blame on women themselves, and mothers in particular. Didn't mothers sign up for whatever misery they experience by deciding to have children in the first place? After all, having kids is a choice.

Yet, in this you-made-your-bed view, motherhood comes at an inexplicably grueling price, almost as a punishment. And children are treated as something akin to puppies—cute little extras we've opted for, perhaps because we find them diverting—rather than as actual people. In what economist Nancy Folbre describes as a children-as-pets mind-set, there's little recognition of the fact that children are essential to society or that keeping them well and ushering them into the era of tax-paying, job-holding adulthood is in the public interest.

Instead, it's simply, "You wanted the cute little thing, now you figure out how to scoop all the poop. And if you can't make a living while doing it, then that, too, is on you."

Blaming women makes a certain sense. No one has to have children. And parents do have some leeway in the decisions they make afterward. Devorah Gartner, for instance, was scrounging around on the floor for change largely because she had quit her job of her own accord. No one had fired her. It can seem that if mothers feel besieged, it's because they've chosen to walk onto the battlefield, to greedily—perhaps selfishly—indulge their weaknesses for chubby cheeks and little toes.

But blaming women for the decisions they make after they have children—as well as for the choice to have children in the first place—doesn't only make women feel bad. It also takes the attention—and, thus, the onus for change—off the real external problems that are causing women's misery.

In 2003, "opting out" entered the lexicon as shorthand for a woman's decision to leave the workplace, and the phenomenon was often discussed as a cultural shift, as if diaper changes and playgroups had suddenly and inexplicably become more rewarding than promotions. The term came from "The Opt-Out Revolution," a *New York Times Magazine* article that was more thoughtful than incendiary, but nevertheless set off a firestorm of chat groups, letters, and editorials. In it, journalist Lisa Belkin wrote about a small group of female Princeton graduates who were choosing to leave their jobs after having children. Belkin's piece largely framed women's retreat from professional life as being on their own terms. "Why don't women run the world?" she asked, and then answered, "Maybe it's because they don't want to."[1]

Although Belkin wasn't advocating that mothers stay at home, her article fed the notion that women had a collective urge to back away from public life. It also helped reinvigorate the old, oversimplified battle between moms who choose to stay at home and those who work full-time. The stay-at-home versus working mother antagonism, or at least this particular chapter in it known as the "mommy wars," had an intensely personal tone, with most installments lauding or blaming individual women for their decisions to either work or not work. Mommy warriors on both sides made the mistake of focusing on the individuals who did the "opting," rather than on the larger forces that affected their choices.

Most people would probably agree that choosing between neglecting a family member in need and making a living is not much of a choice. In her 2006 report "'Opt Out' or Pushed Out?" Joan Williams, a legal scholar and work-life advocate, made this point by drawing attention to the fact that hostile workplace practices often nudge women out of jobs.[2] Nevertheless, choosing, or opting, became the operative concept in the mommy wars. While the literature exhaustively examined the pros and cons of working for money versus staying home with young children, it largely glossed over the fact that even before the economic downturn, the vast majority of mothers could no more casually "opt out" of making money without suffering serious consequences than they could walk away from their children. There's been little mention of the fact that only a small sliver of women were leaving their careers, and they generally were either very well-off, like the Princeton grads in Belkin's story, or paid a high cost for their departure from work, as Devorah Gartner did.

There's been even less attention to the grinding difficulties faced by everyone else: women who face the same work-life stresses as the "opt-out" crowd but can't afford to get out from under them. Instead, the mommy wars took on the tone of a moralistic catfight, in which some women accused other women of making the wrong decisions. Many stay-at-home advocates were openly critical of women who went to work and, more to the point, left their young children in someone's care other than their own. It's an old criticism, and Phyllis Schlafly (interestingly, herself the daughter of a working mother) perhaps put it best back in 1977 when she accused working women of indulging in "a flight from yourself, from responsibility, from the nature of woman, in pursuit of false hopes and fading illusions."[3]

One might expect such finger pointing back then from Schlafly, who was known for her expertise in crafting guilt-inducing rhetoric. But decades later women on both sides of the latest fight are still taking the same tack. Even the latest defenders of working women all too often fault individual women for their decisions, rather than think about the context in which they make them. The retired philosophy professor Linda Hirshman, for instance, took a narrow personal viewpoint in her 2005 essay in the *American Prospect*, which left no question that the issue of women and work was a personal one, based on individual decisions. ("Let's start with you. Educated and affluent reader, if you are a thirty- or fortysomething woman with children, what are you doing? Husbands, what are your wives doing? Older readers, what are your married daughters with children doing?")[4]

Whether their membership is based on working outside the home or staying within it, both clubs have dispiritingly similar messages: boldly defend your "decision," pretend it's worked out perfectly, and blame women who have done otherwise for their choices. Yet for most women, choosing sides isn't that simple. For one thing, despite being pitted against one another, a majority of mothers who work full-time and those who stay home seem to have a similar goal: to be able to take care of their families and earn at least some money. (More on this in chapter 8, on flexible and part-time work.) Indeed, supposed opponents not only often have the same interests, they are sometimes the same people. Take Devorah, who fell on the working mom side of the supposedly great divide before she quit and the next minute, hopes and desires intact, was relegated to the other.

Perhaps the worst part is that the focus on individual women deflected serious examination of the larger family policies, or lack thereof, that affect all women, regardless of their employment status. So, while the fact of the mommy wars spoke to a high level of frustration in both camps, the conversation itself has done little to solve the misery that fueled it. Here women are without any significant help in alleviating their dual responsibilities, yet instead of fighting for the things that might make life easier, we have been fighting and blaming one another.

Many employers seem happy to blame women, too. In workplaces across the country, women have been punished for having responsibilities beyond their job or even for merely seeming as if they might someday have them. Indeed, countless women have been fired or demoted simply for getting pregnant or having children. Yaire Lopez, who drove a truck for Bimbo Bakeries in California, for instance, was fired after her boss learned that she was three months pregnant. A single mom who was already supporting two children with her work, Lopez was so desperate to keep her paycheck that she decided to have an abortion. (Later, when she went to the doctor and learned she was carrying twins, she changed her mind and left her job.)[5] In Madison, Wisconsin, Tracy Lust, a mattress salesperson, was passed over for a promotion "because you have kids," as her boss told her.[6]

Meanwhile, a pregnant Shireen Walsh found herself showered with hostility, rather than baby gifts, in her Minneapolis office. Walsh, who sold and renewed service contracts on scanners at the National Computer Systems Company, developed borderline gestational diabetes during pregnancy and had to ask for time off to go to the doctor. Although her condition soon stabilized, from that point on, Walsh felt antagonism radiating from her boss, who scrutinized Walsh's hours; referred to Walsh's son as "the sickling" because he suffered from violent allergic reactions; and tacked "Out—Sick Child" signs up in Walsh's office when she had to stay home with him. On one occasion, after Walsh fainted in the office because of the stress, her boss stopped by her cubicle to warn her that she "better not be pregnant again." She wasn't—but she left the job anyway.[7]

As much as these women needed and wanted their income, the problem goes well beyond the simple loss of jobs and money. Workers in these situations are often the targets of palpable anger, as if their efforts to both work and care for children are not simply a potential obstacle to business, but a deliberate affront to the gender order. You can hear the free-floating nastiness seep out in the reprimand Devorah Gartner received for asking for time off. It's there, too, in the condescending comments from Tracy Lust's boss, who regularly made "blonde barbs" (as in "You're being a blonde again today") and asked why Lust's husband, Jerry, "wasn't going to take care" of her. In Minneapolis, Walsh's boss even threw a phone book at her desk once, demanding that Walsh find a pediatrician who was open after work hours.

Yet even when projectiles are flying at their heads, or, perhaps, *particularly* when projectiles are flying at their heads, most people are so focused on ducking, they're unlikely to absorb the fact that their problems extend far beyond them. While it may be impossible not to take such an assault personally, the hostility toward Walsh is connected to the anger directed toward other mothers—indeed, toward caretakers of all sorts.

Although men are less likely to get caught in the phone-book crossfire mentioned previously (because they're less likely to be responsible for a sick child), it's clear that when they do take on the care of others, they can incite a variation of the fury and bigotry that female workers are more likely to encounter. Take Howard Kevin Knussman, a state trooper in Maryland who requested family medical leave to care for his newborn child when his wife had postpartum complications. His supervisor, who happened to be a woman, not only denied Knussman's request, she also told him that "God made women to have babies." Because he was a man, she said, his wife would have to be "in a coma or dead" before he could be given primary caregiver status and the family medical leave that goes with it.[8]

How could any employee hope to keep it all together in the face of such outright resistance toward accommodating the realities of life? To reinforce the idea that it's possible to be at once highly responsible to a family and to a job that makes little to no accommodations for family, we have the regularly resurrected myth of "Supermom," someone who does it all, preferably while also training for marathons and looking really good in public, or at least retaining her composure.

Although Sarah Palin wasn't the first and won't be the last, the Republican vice-presidential candidate was one of the most prominent women recently cast in the Supermom role. At least at first, right after her running mate, John McCain, introduced her to the country as a "devoted wife and mother of five," it seemed like she might pull it off. She appealed as a potential Juggler in Chief, who might show what women could achieve with the right mix of professional opportunity and agreeable life partner. Clearly, she had personal experience with some of the challenges American women care most about: mothering special-needs children, balancing work with new motherhood, and teen pregnancy.

Ultimately, serious questions about her competence (along with the collapse of both the economy and the McCain campaign) were responsible for undermining Palin's candidacy. An electorate thirsty for change decided fairly quickly that on matters of foreign policy, all things financial, as well as the work-life issues close to women's hearts, she had only traditional Republican fixes to offer and not even a particularly good grasp of those. But even as her failings on matters of substance sent her approval ratings tumbling, her symbolic value was undergoing its own, arguably more riveting, collapse.

Even though Palin had clearly been picked and groomed to appeal to women, discomfiting personal details emerged to seriously undermine the idea of her as "Supermom." Somehow, the plain, ordinary "hockey mom," as she called herself, had kept her pregnant daughter out of school for long stretches; had hidden her own unplanned pregnancy from family members and colleagues; had stayed in a governors' meeting despite being in labor; and had returned to work three days after giving birth to a special-needs infant. While bloggers were gleefully delving into uncomfortable personal questions (Whose baby was it, really? Did Palin know her daughter was pregnant before she decided to run? Was it fair to expose her pregnant daughter to worldwide scrutiny?), the question of real significance to the rest of American women went unasked: what does it mean for ordinary women if a woman whose life is managed by teams of professionals has this hard a time balancing work and family?

Conversations about Supermoms such as Palin usually involve much marveling about their being "so organized!" and "so efficient!" which, no doubt, they must be to keep so many balls in the air. Yet too often this effusiveness masks the nitty-gritty financial details of how high-profile women really manage. These mythic dynamos often have either a paid support system that most women can't afford or stay-at-home family members (or, in the case of Sarah Palin, both). These are perfectly reasonable ways to handle domestic responsibilities, of course. But to pretend that these supports don't exist is to set up women who don't have them for both failure and, yes, blame.

This was the problem with picking Sarah Palin for the Republican presidential ticket (one that will likely resurface should she still be in the party's graces in 2012). She was a symbolic, rather than a substantive, answer to women's very real problems. (Try as you might, you simply can't craft national policy that will grant everyone a high-paying job and a Todd Palin equivalent. And, most women probably wouldn't want that anyway.) On top of that, Palin, or, at least her image-crafters, left a lot of women feeling bad about themselves. If she can raise five kids, govern a state, and still have time to shop and bag the occasional moose, then what's wrong with the rest of us?

Therein lies the terrible power of the Supermom myth, what makes it both so damaging and so enduring. It lives on by hooking into women's self-doubt, keeping them from looking outward while they desperately scramble to find the time to do everything. The impossible quest to be just a bit more organized or try a little harder helps explain the fact that both single and married working mothers typically sleep less than six hours a night, according to a 2006 survey of the National Sleep Foundation. (The survey also found that 44 percent of full-time working mothers with school-aged children felt too tired to have sex.)[9] In the meantime, the myth has spawned a host of products aimed at the exhausted and overextended mom, including the recent crop of energy drinks for women, such as Pink, Her, and Go Girl.

In truth, of course, no matter how much get-up-and-go or caffeine anyone can harness, really shouldering "it all" is usually impossible without enough help or the money to buy it. Nevertheless, many women have accepted responsibility for their untenable situations, if not by consciously embracing it, then by internalizing the disapproval of others, so that a layer of guilt compounds their external stresses. Take Amy Van Ry, a fund-raiser and mother of two in New York City, who told me she was literally sickened when she realized she was going to be late to pick up her eight-year-old son Sterling from his after-school program. "I felt like I was going to barf," was how she put it, hours after the incident. Because she works full-time, Van Ry only occasionally picks her son up in the afternoon—and then, with much wrangling of her schedule beforehand. The rest of the time, either a babysitter or her husband gets Sterling. For some reason, she had forgotten to enter her responsibility into her electronic calendar that day.

Van Ry realized her error just as the after-school program was ending, but it was still too late to get there on time. With rush-hour traffic, it would take her at least half an hour to reach the school where the program was housed. Even if she abandoned her e-mail mid-sentence, called a car service, and ran maniacally out of her office—all of which she immediately did—she knew she would be late.

There would be financial consequences, as she had learned from the two other times she had been late to pick up Sterling in the year he had been at after-school. The program requires parents to pay fifteen dollars for every ten minutes past pick-up time. The fee, along with twenty dollars she paid for the car service, would take a painful bite out of their moderate income. Yet no matter how much she owed, the emotional toll was greater.

By the time she arrived at the school thirty minutes and sixty-five dollars later, both her son and the after-school program director were furious at her. It was as if the towering man in his forties and her wiry, blond-haired boy were competing to see who could make her feel worse. Because of Amy, the director was going to be late to pick up his own daughter from day care, he informed her. His statement, uttered through clenched teeth, sent a fresh stab of guilt into her belly. Sterling was equally effective. The last lone child on the curb outside the school, he greeted her with a quivering chin that quickly gave way to full-bore crying. "Don't ever make me go to after-school again," he sobbed accusingly.

Although Van Ry told me she wanted to "curl up in a ball and die" after the episode, it's possible that what she really wanted was not to juggle so many responsibilities each day or at least have more help with them. When asked whether she would be interested in a job with flexible hours that would make it easier to pick up Sterling or perhaps just a little extra wiggle room in both her and her husband's work schedule or a school bus that might drop Sterling directly at home, she chuckled bitterly, as if only a fool could hope for such extravagances. And, at least that night, she didn't have the time to dream about them. She had to write a letter of apology to the director of the after-school program and make amends to her son.

To borrow from the language of addiction, admitting there is a problem is the first step in solving it. In the case of American families, the challenge is not so much copping to the fact that things aren't working. Even the most sleep-deprived, addled mom will tell you there's a problem when she doesn't have enough money for diapers or that something's at least a bit off when her agony over being late to pick up her child reaches stomach-clutching proportions.

The challenge for American women is seeing the problem as bigger than their own families.

Like Amy Van Ry, wracked by guilt to the point of nausea, most of the women I spoke with for this book seemed to accept their unhappiness as their own—theirs to endure and, because few considered alternative culprits, presumably of their own, or maybe their partners', creation. Perhaps because so many were sleepless, overworked, and juggling responsibilities, they were too consumed with getting through the day to see a bigger picture. Or maybe it was a lack of exposure to real, potential alternatives to their situations that made it so difficult for them to imagine anything better for themselves.

. . .

Growing up in Romania under the harsh communist regime of Nicolae Ceauşescu, Maria Nistor could have counted on one hand the number of times she'd tasted chocolate. She'd eaten bananas at most twice a year. Her entire family had regularly woken up at three in the morning to get in a long line of people waiting for milk. And she and everyone around her had dreamed of coming to the United States. In some ways, her dream went as planned: In her early twenties, she moved to Savannah, Georgia, and got a job as a loan officer at a credit union. She met and married a nice tennis instructor. They settled in a modest home on the outskirts of the city, and she soon found herself pregnant with twins.

Yet after she gave birth, just when she should have been entering the happily-ever-after stage of her dream, Nistor found herself instead staying awake all night worrying about health insurance. Just two weeks into her maternity leave, she had received a letter from her employer threatening to cut off her—and, by extension, her family's—benefits, unless she returned to work only two weeks after bearing twins by cesarean section. Ultimately, after begging her boss for mercy, Nistor was able to keep her health insurance, and she stayed home for an additional four weeks of unpaid maternity leave. But from that point on, she felt as if her bosses treated her as suspect. Indeed, less than a year later, she was fired after missing work to spend the day with her infant daughter, who had been hospitalized with a respiratory problem. Just as Nistor had arrived at work from her daughter's bedside, ready to work despite her exhaustion, her supervisor approached. Although he knew her daughter was sick, he didn't ask after the child's health before dropping the ax.

Among the horror stories of working parents I heard while researching this book, Nistor's wasn't particularly awful. Despite falling into a depression that left her temporarily bed-bound and unable to function immediately after being fired, within months she had found another job. (Because she didn't tell her present employer about her past difficulties, she chose to go by her middle name here.) Her children's health gradually improved, and her marriage somehow survived the ordeal intact.

In researching this book, I met and interviewed dozens of people in equally and even more upsetting situations, if you can directly compare such things. Many of them hadn't landed as squarely on their feet as Maria Nistor had, yet most weren't nearly as outraged. In contrast, Maria Nistor was furious about how she was treated as a working mother. After being fired, Nistor even began to think about returning to the country she had fled. Perhaps Romania's biggest draw was that Nistor harbored no illusions about her homeland; she had always known it as a place of hardship and turmoil. The United States was supposed to be different.

Ironically, her response seems in part due to having grown up in a foreign country that, while notoriously harsh, still provided for essentials. Indeed, lack of chocolate and civil rights aside, even the Romania of Nistor's youth in many ways seemed like a better place to raise children. "At least there, I always knew I'd have health insurance and be able to take care of my family," she recently said about her life before immigrating. And, perhaps because she had grown up there, she knew that her situation here could and should be different—and that it wasn't her fault.

3

'Til Dishes Do Us Part

The Problem with Blaming Men

Perhaps, then, the fault lies with men. Erika Escobedo certainly thinks so. Less than two days after she returned from the hospital where she had given birth to her third child, Escobedo found herself mopping her kitchen floor. "I had him at 8:13 a.m., and I came home from the hospital the next morning," she recalls, not fondly. By the afternoon, she was back on her feet, mop in hand. "I hadn't slept in thirty-six hours, but I went home and cleaned my house anyway."

How does any woman wind up doing menial labor so soon after enduring labor of the other sort? Escobedo, a thirty-six-year-old mother of three boys who lives in Huntington Beach, California, insists that she had no choice. She knew that neither cajoling nor rational argument would convince her husband to pick up the mop. Although she ought to have been asleep in bed or perhaps propped in a comfortable chair nursing her newborn, there was a brown, sticky puddle smack in the middle of her kitchen floor—and there it would have remained, she says, had she not gotten out of bed to clean it.

Two years and many bottles of Pine-Sol after that postpartum mopping bout, Escobedo, who now works full-time as a receptionist at an appraisal company, still finds herself solely responsible for all of the housework, in addition to most child-related tasks. "I'm doing the laundry, cooking, doing the dishes, cleaning, dropping my son off at day care, going to the grocery store," she says. "If I'm not at work, I am literally either cleaning or doing household chores."

And her husband's contribution? "Sometimes he'll kick the dirty clothes to the laundry area," says Escobedo. "He doesn't even wipe the counter. He spilled a beer a couple of days ago, and when I came home at night, that spot of beer was still there." Nor do her sons—Steel, Stone, and Striker—help much around the house, according to Escobedo. Being only two years old, Striker can be forgiven. But his older brothers are ten and twelve and still don't do any chores.

The division of domestic labor among adults in heterosexual couples has improved over the last generation or two but not enough to keep pace with the other changes in women's lives. Since 1965, men have almost tripled the amount of time they spend with their children and more than doubled the number of hours they devote to housework.[1] And both men and women seem to have a growing awareness that housework is a crucial component of romantic relationships. A 2007 survey done by the Pew Research Center found that "sharing household chores" now ranks third in importance among criteria for successful marriages among both men and women, following faithfulness and a "happy sexual relationship."[2]

Yet despite the fact that most mothers now work full-time, they still often bear the brunt of domestic chores. Women do 63 percent of the household work—twice what men do. That amounts to almost sixteen hours per week of cleaning and making food, as opposed to men, who put in less than ten hours weekly on these tasks, according to 2007 data from the Bureau of Labor Statistics. What's more, men's contribution to household chores, while significantly greater than it was in the 1960s, has stalled recently, with their input remaining more or less consistent over the last twenty years. Several studies have found that even married couples that identify as egalitarian often don't truly divide housework equally.[3]

Given the lag in men's assumption of housework, it's easy to see how they can appear to be the root of women's overburden. And sometimes, as in Escobedo's case, they may be. Certainly, the fact that most married working women still do more housework and child care than their male partners do has taken a grave toll on women and their relationships.

Beyond simply not helping, some men add to the household workload.[4] This is Emigh Allison's complaint. An administrative assistant at a homeless shelter in Easton, Pennsylvania, Allison has an eight-year-old daughter from a brief previous marriage, whom she raised on her own for several years before she met her current husband. Although she says it was in many ways more difficult to be a single mother, Allison is nostalgic for the relationship to cleaning she used to have in her former life. "When it was just me and my daughter, I knew what state my house was in when I left. I knew what was needed in the evening," she says. "Now, when I come home, I don't know what mess is waiting for me."

As much as the uneven splitting of chores often leaves women holding the bag, or mop, there is more to such domestic imbalances than just individual laziness or ineptitude. Certainly couples need to try to address the inequities within their relationships, which, unchecked, can ruin and end them. But squabbles over housework shouldn't distract us from trying to resolve the larger issues that affect both men and women.

What happens when women add the lion's share of the housework and child care to their hours spent earning money? Where does the time come from? Having long since cut back on pleasant but arguably unnecessary pastimes, such as spending time with friends and reading, many women have moved on to sacrifice sleep and physical exercise. More than half of the 1,003 women surveyed by the National Sleep Foundation said that when they were pressed for time, sleep and exercise, in that order, were the first two things to be jettisoned.

Clearly, whether or not they get a good night's sleep, cleaning the house in addition to putting in a full day of work and a full evening of child care leaves many women feeling tapped out or "deeply, deeply, deeply exhausted," as Andrea M., the mother of five-year-old twin boys and an eighteen-month-old daughter, puts it. To her and perhaps also to her colleagues' dismay, Andrea often falls asleep in meetings, despite her impressive intake of coffee and the highly caffeinated Red Bull energy drink.

A petite woman with long, brown hair and a wide smile, Andrea is a food scientist in Rockford, Illinois, who works full-time managing product development for a company that makes rice crackers and sesame sticks. At work, she has a team of several employees with whom she shares responsibilities. When she gets home, though, she mostly goes solo, single-handedly tackling caretaking chores not only for her small children, but also for her messy house. After she puts the kids to bed around eight o'clock., Andrea usually cleans until well past midnight. "There's laundry and diapers and pizza boxes to deal with," she explains. "Every day it's like an explosion when I come home."

Andrea's husband runs a small company that does DJing for parties, which means he often works nights and is available to care for the children during the day. But although Andrea says her husband is a fun and loving dad, he is also "the biggest slob you've ever seen in your life," or, to put it another way, "the human tornado." In her descriptions of the scenes she typically encounters upon returning from work, her husband comes off like a cross between Mary Poppins and Pigpen. "The children are thrilled to be with him. A lot of times those boys are running around the house, and they're into everything, and they're making tents and everything. Then he'll change the baby and throw the dirty diaper on the floor."

Andrea's "second shift," as sociologist Arlie Hochschild has called the time women put in doing housework after returning home from their jobs, is not only hard on her body and her professional life, it's become a cloud over her marriage, too. "I'm resentful a lot," she says, describing a recent weekend morning on which her husband slept late. ("I can't remember the last time I slept eleven hours," she observes with a bitter chuckle.) Then he got up and proceeded to lie on the couch. Eventually, he ate breakfast, cooked by Andrea, after which he put his plate on top of the kids' dirty ones in the sink and left to browse the Internet. "How can you look at a dirty kitchen and not think to help?" asks Andrea, who says the frustration she feels with her husband can dampen her affection for him. "It makes me feel bad when I make an effort to clean everything up and have it nice when I feel he doesn't care. You don't want him touching you."

Tensions over the division of domestic work often affect the rest of a marriage, as they have in Andrea and her husband's case. Overwork is a huge problem for both men and women, with one in three employees chronically having too much to do, according to a 2005 report by the Families and Work Institute.[5] Add the struggles over housework and child care, and marriage becomes both less pleasant and less stable. Women who do more housework than their partners do are more likely to fantasize about divorce.[6] And whether or not their perceptions are accurate, women who feel as if they're doing more than their share of housework are also more likely to end their unsatisfying marriages, according to a 2003 article published in the *Journal of Family Issues*.[7] Conversely, wives are more sexually interested in husbands who take on more household responsibilities.[8]

On a recent evening in the Mercer household, there was little chance of sex. Even the possibility of cordial conversation had been pretty much vanquished by the escalating tensions between Ann and her husband. While their three-year-old daughter, Giselle, miraculously slept in the next room, her parents warred loudly over who would stay home with her the next day. Because she had a fever, Giselle (who, like Ann, is referred to here by her middle, rather than first, name) couldn't attend preschool the next day, so one of the parents would have to stay home with her. Ann, an interior designer who runs her own business, pointed out that if she had to stay home with Giselle, she would be forced to further delay deadlines for finishing two projects and would likely anger her clients. Her husband, an art preparation technician who works at a museum, said that he risked being fired if he called in sick. "Someone's going to have to stay home," Ann finally shouted. After this statement of the obvious, she hurled a spoon in frustration, which bounced off the counter top, leaving an impressive nick in the butcher block—and a less than romantic ambience in the room. For a moment that seemed like an eternity, both Ann and her husband silently let their eyes rest on the small dent.

"It wasn't just anger at him; it was at his employers and the situation," she said the next day, when slightly more level heads prevailed.

But even with some cooling-off time, Ann still has a bleak assessment of her marriage. The stress of trying to stay afloat while raising a child and maintaining their careers has pushed Ann and her husband near the breaking point before. The two went for an entire year without having sex when their daughter was one. They considered divorce last year but decided that, at least for the moment, it would be financially unwise.

"We'd both end up destitute," she says with a bitter laugh.

Together, the couple makes just enough to cover their rent and the basics. But every month some new expense seems to crop up, be it child care or medical bills, that sets the family finances back. Somehow, in their daughter's three short years of life, they have amassed more than $100,000 dollars in debt, even though Ann has at times babysat another child for extra cash, while running her own business out of her home and caring for Giselle. With the juggling of bills, work, and child care, the two partners have little time to see each other. Too often, when they are together, things go in the projectile-hurling direction. And now Ann is pregnant again.

Not getting enough help with child-rearing can not only make women miserable, it can also bring on measurable, diagnosable illness. So great is the strain on women who single-handedly shoulder the responsibility of looking after their children that they have more than three times the risk of developing mental health problems, compared with their peers who feel adequately supported, according to a 2007 study of 1,747 mothers.[9] Participants who reported having no one to rely on for day-to-day emotional support in parenting had triple the risk of poor mental health as did those who had support. Mothers who lacked support and had two or more additional "parenting stressors," such as difficulty paying for things their children need or feeling that they were spending too much or too little time with their children, had a nearly twelvefold increased risk for developing mental health problems, such as depression, according to the study.

This gendered split over work within many households may be the biggest divide holding up the progress of women and entire families, as members fight each other instead of taking on the external problems that hinder them as a unit. (Just imagine if every utensil hurled at a spouse were instead a letter fired off to a legislator, demanding paid sick days that could be used to care for a sick child. . . .) But even with women's progress, gender equity, and domestic harmony at stake, it's impossible to bridge the housework divide without understanding why, with women already so well integrated into the workplace, cleaning and child care have yet to be more evenly divided within male-female couples.

No doubt some of the explanation lies in the more than two-hundred-year history of men being the primary or sole breadwinners in the United States and the even longer history of women shouldering the responsibility for domestic work. Researchers have studied the various ways that both men and women within couples fall into and perpetuate these traditional roles, making decisions both at work and at home that dig them further into their entrenched positions. All the while, they're not only "doing gender," as sociologists like to call the collection of interactions that creates their roles, they're also passing their behaviors on to the next generation by showing their children how to behave within their own future relationships.

Thus, when asked to explain the lopsided division of straightening, wiping, and diaper changing in their lives, many women often talk about their mothers-in-law. Erika Escobedo, the woman in California who wound up mopping on her first day home from the hospital, lays the blame for her husband's outright refusal to share in the housework squarely at the feet of his mother. Escobedo's mother-in-law stayed home with her sons and "babied their booties," as she puts it, until the boys grew into men, married, and left her house. Even when Escobedo's mother-in-law was diagnosed with cancer and had only a few more months to live, she continued to cook and clean for her family.

Although Erika works full-time, she says she feels her husband expects her to perform the same level of housework that his mother did. Escobedo wasn't the only overworked mother I spoke with who described this sort of generational lag, in which husbands' expectations remained based on their own mothers who hadn't worked outside the home. Such deep social grooves regarding housework are incredibly difficult, though not impossible, to escape. Erika and Mike Escobedo have regularly argued about housework for years, with Erika alternately begging her husband to help and furiously raging at his refusal to do so. She even occasionally goes "on strike," as she puts it, refusing to do any housework until she gets so disgusted with the state of her house that she calls the strike off herself. She has also tried to compel her older children to help out. "I've said, 'Stone, you do not want to become a loser. Losers do not do anything for themselves.'" But nothing seems to help.

To the extent that the problem lies in how children are raised, the solution would seem simple—at least for the next generation: parents could break the cycle by setting an example, sharing housework and paid work so that their children can follow in their footsteps. Emigh Allison in Pennsylvania, who lives with her daughter, her new husband, and a son she had with him, hoped to do just that. "I just really didn't want my children to get the idea that because you are a woman, you're stuck with these chores," she says. So she and her husband came up with a list of all the housework that needed to be done and divided it evenly between them. The only problem with this Solomonic solution was that after a few days, her husband stopped doing his assigned share of the work. So now Allison does his tasks in addition to her own, although she's careful to wait until her children go to sleep to do his, so as to preserve the illusion of gender equity in the household.

Because not all men are housework-challenged—some, of course, do their share of cooking, cleaning, child care, and plenty more—women should perhaps size up their partners' domestic failings before they marry them and choose more helpful husbands. But it's not always that easy. Even slobs are more likely to help around the house during the courtship period, according to recent research based on data from more than seventeen thousand people. Apparently, men do more housework as live-in boyfriends than they do after marriage, when they tend to morph into stereotypical unhelpful husbands.[10]

In Escobedo's case, for instance, she learned about her husband's domestic helplessness only when it was, as she puts it, "too late." When they were dating, she knew that Mike would often swing by his mother's house; she just didn't know why. "When I finally realized he was going to pick up his laundry, I went, 'Oh, shit, he's one of those guys,'" Escobedo recalls. "But by then, I was already pregnant."

No doubt, everyone's on his or her best behavior before "sealing the deal," as it were. But expedience aside, larger circumstances, shaped by laws and policy, also affect how men and women divide housework and child care. It's not that the government can directly cause or solve these intra-marital struggles exactly. But the converse of the old feminist axiom that "the personal is political" seems to apply: laws and regulations deeply affect how families function day to day. In other words, the political—or policy that comes out of the political, anyway—has deep personal ramifications. In the case of American families, the influential force is a dearth of family-friendly laws and regulations that could help ease the double burden of paid work and caring. By not instituting such supports, the government has created an increasingly grueling reality for male and female American workers, which has in turn made it especially hard for many heterosexual couples to break out of their patterns.

Indeed, due in large part to weak and nonexistent government regulations of employers, the lives of all workers have gotten considerably more demanding in recent years. So, although many women have entered the workforce, a change that would be expected to make their partners' lives easier by increasing family income and perhaps allowing them to work less, in fact, most men are facing harsher working conditions. The extra income has gone to pay for the fast-growing costs of housing, child care, health care, and college tuition, rather than providing a cushier life for families.[11] Meanwhile, workplace stress levels in the United States have doubled since 1985, with one-third of all people saying that job stress is the single greatest stressor in their life.[12]

The American workweek is now the longest in the industrialized world, with workers putting in 180 hours more per year now than they did twenty years ago.[13] Workers in the United States are on the job the equivalent of almost two work weeks longer than even their notoriously workaholic counterparts in Japan, according to the International Labor Organization. There are few breaks from this constant pressure. Twenty-eight million Americans, or one in four working in the private sector, get no paid vacation or paid holidays at all.[14] Interestingly, women are less likely to have paid vacation benefits, with one-third of women, as opposed to a quarter of men, having no paid vacation benefits.[15] In contrast to the 127 countries that have laws that protect workers' rights to paid vacation, the United States has no vacation policy.[16]

During the last two decades as work pressures have been steadily climbing, men's wages have been just as steadily dropping. The wages of married men with a college education or less have fallen 8 percent in the last twenty-seven years, according to Jared Bernstein, the author of *Crunch: Why Do I Feel So Squeezed?* and the chief economic advisor to Vice President Joe Biden.[17]

The increased pressures on men in the workplace have undoubtedly made the prospect of pitching in at home even less appealing. Consider, again, Mike Escobedo. Surely, one of the central stresses of his marriage to Erika is that the two harbor very different ideas about gender roles. You could even accuse him of doing as little as he can get away with. And there's little doubt that at least as Erika describes it (I tried, but failed, to speak with Mike directly), she has wound up with the short end of the stick.

Still, while not letting Mike Escobedo entirely off the hook, there's also a more charitable explanation of his behavior. Assuming he is "one of those guys," as his wife claims, part of the reason may be that his life is at least as hard as, if not harder than, his father's was. Despite having high blood pressure, Escobedo puts in long hours as a laborer, often arriving at the construction sites where he works by 5 a.m. After fifteen years of doing this kind of work, he is striving to become a foreman, which means working even harder.

So it's somewhat understandable that Mike Escobedo, who grew up watching his mother wait on his hardworking father, might expect the same treatment from Erika when he gets home from a grueling day of physical labor. He is exhausted and overworked. The problem is that Erika, who has a full-time job herself, is exhausted and overworked, too. Indeed, while women's paid work lives are subject to the same increasing stresses as men's, many women have incomprehensibly also added to the amount of time they spend doing child care. Working women now log even more time doing child care than stay-at-home mothers did in 1975, according to sociologist Suzanne Bianchi, who has extensively studied couples' time use patterns.[18]

Emerging research on the more than six hundred thousand same-sex families in the United States helps establish that difficulties sharing responsibility for a household are not unique to male-female couples. Perhaps not surprisingly, the mounting data does show that same-sex couples tend to share housework and child care more fairly than heterosexual ones do. No doubt this is partly due to the fact that same-sex couples don't have the same deeply grooved husband-and-wife patterns to fall into. Lesbians with children have a better record of dividing both domestic and earning responsibilities. And both lesbians and gay men are less likely to wind up economically dependent on a partner.[19]

Yet lesbians and gay men still often struggle over the division of household labor.[20] Their difficulties speak to the near impossibility of dividing responsibilities when there are simply too many of them, gender breakdowns aside. Money, or how the earning of it is divided within a couple, is often deeply tied to how that couple shares housework. There is some evidence that among same-sex couples, the number of hours respondents spent in paid labor outside of the home predicts the percentage of the tasks they were responsible for within it. Within heterosexual couples, of course, the same relationship holds, with men typically both doing less housework and earning more than women, even when both partners work full-time. (Full-time, salaried working women earn only 80 percent of what their male equivalents did in 2007.)[21]

You could argue that there is a certain justness in having the amount of household work a man does correspond to his wife's financial contributions: the bigger her paycheck, the more loads of laundry he should put in. Yet the reality is more complicated. For one, men still do less domestic work when their wives earn the same amount they do. Then, too, earning more doesn't necessarily mean working harder. Low-paying jobs can be more stressful, time-consuming, and difficult than higher-paying jobs.

Although career imbalances seem to lead to household imbalances, splitting all of the paid work and the family caring perfectly down the middle isn't necessarily the solution—or at least an easy or pleasant one.

Tag-team parenting, one of the most common answers to both the gender-equity dilemma and the high cost of child care and after-school care, can present serious challenges to marriages.

Some one-third of families rely on this arrangement, in which both parents stagger their schedules so that one can be home with young children while the other works. But partners who split their time this way see each other less and run a greater risk of divorce. Families in which one spouse works overnight and the other works days are as much as six times more likely to divorce than couples who don't have this arrangement, according to Harriet Presser, a sociology professor at the University of Maryland–College Park, who studied more than thirty-four hundred couples.[22]

For Heather Steinbrink of Erie, Pennsylvania, the problem with tag-team parenting wasn't so much that she and her husband—who worked different, though overlapping shifts—didn't get along; it was that they didn't have much of a relationship of any sort. When Steinbrink returned to her job as a retail pharmacist after a three-month maternity leave in the summer of 2003, she was working ten-hour days in a drugstore and her husband was teaching mechanical engineering full-time at a university. Most days, Steinbrink worked from 9 a.m. until 7 p.m. and her husband would pick up their daughter at child care around 4:30 p.m. On rare occasions, Heather was able to stay home on a weekday. But in exchange for this day off, she had to work all day Saturday and a half-day on Sunday. If they were lucky, the couple spent one hour together before going to sleep on weekday nights.

"We usually had a fairly hurried meal, and then it was just on to dealing with the kids and getting ready for the next day," recalls Steinbrink. And though the two at least set eyes on each other every day, they were of little comfort to each other and were steadily drifting further apart. "I felt very lonely," says Steinbrink. "When we were finally together, he was too tired to talk and so was I. We just weren't together enough to make a real connection."

So, shortly after her second child was born, after a year and a half of trading shifts with fellow pharmacists and struggling to find time with her husband and children, Steinbrink quit her job. To make ends meet, the family sold their second car and cut back on extra expenses like travel, eating out, clothes shopping, and movies. In many ways, Steinbrink prefers these sacrifices to the ones she had made to work full-time, but her career prospects are now very much up in the air. She's taking classes in accounting, with plans to eventually start her own business, although she is unsure when or how that will happen.

Women's careers are often the first to either be scaled back or cut entirely. Perhaps the husband earns more, so it's important not to endanger his job. Or the husband is happy to take responsibility for the finances, while the wife wants to be more involved with child care. Or the couple simply drifted into the arrangement. Jessica DeGroot has heard all of these answers and more. The founder of ThirdPath, an organization that supports men and women who want to share work and parenting, DeGroot has counseled dozens of unhappy couples who found that the traditional work-family path has led them to unhappiness. "Men feel nagged, women feel unsupported," says DeGroot, who sees these traditional gender roles often gradually sneaking up on couples after they have children. Typically, both partners have a part in imposing the roles, with women sacrificing some or all work responsibilities to take on greater control at home, while men's careers balloon to the point of not permitting them much time to parent or do housework.

ThirdPath is only one of the groups that has sprung up to guide couples through the tricky process of bucking entrenched work-life traditions. Marc and Amy Vachon, who both work thirty-two hours a week and equally split care for their two children and housework, also evenly divide responsibility for Equally Shared Parenting, a joint project that promotes the gospel of household balance. While ThirdPath has created a network of career and couples counselors and highlights the accomplishments of workers who have achieved success within their careers while carving out time for their families, the Vachons are getting the word out through a Web site devoted to shared parenting, a guidebook on the subject, and by example. Their saga was told in a *New York Times Magazine* cover story that was published on Mother's Day 2008. After detailing Marc Vachon's long search for a job that would accommodate his need for a part-time schedule, the article ended with Marc, having secured a good, flexible job, tiptoeing out of his new office earlier than most employees to go home and hold down the fort.

It's an inspiring image. A solid-looking guy with a friendly face and thinning blondish hair, Vachon is clearly a sterling example of a man who wants to pull his domestic weight. But his success is a qualified one. Even with his enthusiasm and clarity of purpose, Marc Vachon had to go to near-Herculean measures to find a company willing to accommodate his interest in sharing household responsibilities. A gifted job applicant with a mechanical engineering degree, he still had a hard time locating companies willing to accommodate his need for flexibility. And after he found an understanding employer, he was very much the exception—so much so, that tiptoeing out of the office was necessary, lest he piss off his colleagues with less-flexible schedules.

ThirdPath and the Vachons are doing important work, slowly changing the culture by working with individual families who want to break out of old patterns. Yet there's only so much even the most earnest and well-meaning individual man, woman, or organization can do without laws and regulations that will make family life more livable for U.S. workers. Until employers are required to accommodate the family responsibilities of their male and female workers with good part-time and flexible work options, paid sick leave, and vacations, people like Marc Vachon will have to continue going to absurd lengths to share domestic work. And many others who aren't quite so indispensable to employers will never have the privilege of tiptoeing out the door.

To get the kind of work situation that would ease the burden on all workers with domestic responsibilities—be they female or male, married or single, parents or childless—and, in turn, help facilitate domestic peace, we'd need a broad demand for workplace changes. Unfortunately, the issue suffers from a sort of categorical catch-22. Most of the scholars and advocates who have devoted themselves to improving the balance between work and family are women. The dilemma of how to both earn money and do caring work crops up in women's studies courses, women's forums, and even the congressional women's caucus. Framing work-family issues as women's problems is a natural outgrowth of the fact that women feel most burdened by, and thus care most about, them. Yet labeling these issues "women's" excludes, or at least doesn't necessarily welcome, people who are essential to solving them: men.

If more men do take on greater domestic responsibilities, they'll likely soon see the need for the broader structural changes that many female advocates have been pushing. That's because men who buck traditional gender roles often wind up being treated like women. Remember Kevin Knussman, the state trooper who couldn't get time off to care for his newborn even when his wife was sick and was told that "unless your wife is in a coma or dead, you can't be the primary care provider?" Chris Schultz, a male maintenance worker, met with a similar level of understanding when he took time off to do what women have more traditionally done. His employer, the Advocate Health and Hospitals Corporation, fired him when he returned from leave spent caring for his dying mother and demented father.[23]

Indeed, more and more men are already facing so-called family responsibilities discrimination in the workplace when they seek to actively care for their children or other family members. According to the Hastings Center for WorkLife

Law, which specializes in such cases, men increasingly have trouble getting accurate information from employers about leave and benefits. They are discouraged from taking leave to which they are entitled. And if they do take family leave, they often find that they get paid back in the form of bad assignments, job transfers, or exclusion from important business networks.

Perhaps that explains part of our rut: men realize that taking on more work at home will likely mean inviting sacrifices and struggles at work. Yet, hopefully, there are payoffs, too. When men ask Marc Vachon of Equally Shared Parenting what they get in exchange for doing domestic work, he likes to tell them that the tasks, or at least the time spent doing them, become their own reward. Even if fathers don't like changing their children's diapers, simply being together can facilitate a stronger and more fulfilling relationship between them, he argues. For those who remain unconvinced—perhaps Mike Escobedo would fall into this category—Vachon says that pitching in around the house offers another, likely more enticing payoff: a much, much happier partner.

4

The Problems We Wish We Had

A Couple of Choices, None of Them Good

There was a popular boom-time story line about women. It usually focused on a high-earning mother, who was torn in some way between career and children, and whose problems now seem about as pressing as an investment banker's. Consider a few of the women profiled in Leslie Bennetts's 2007 book *The Feminine Mistake: Are We Giving Up Too Much?*, which weighed in on the women-should-work side of the mommy wars debate.[1] There's Susan Yardley, or at least the mother given that pseudonym, whose husband "earns a seven-figure income that pays for their children's expensive private school education as well as the family's luxury co-op apartment and their weekend house in the Hamptons." Clearly, Bennetts is referring to an extremely narrow demographic when she describes Yardley as a poster mom of sorts: "the quintessential chic Manhattan wife—whippet thin and sinewy, her auburn hair artfully colored and fashionably tousled."

Then there's Donna Chatsworth, who enjoys "a four-bedroom New York apartment, a country estate in northwestern Connecticut, children in expensive private school, and lavish vacations to exotic destinations." And Wendy Greenberg, a woman with a Harvard law degree who chose not to reveal her real name to readers (perhaps because she feared she would come off as ridiculously privileged). Bennetts describes Greenberg's annual holiday party, which features "a staggering array of baked goodies piled on fancy tiered trays and artfully heaped on expensive platters, a display so lavish it could easily be immortalized as a gorgeous magazine cover depicting holiday extravagance at its most impressive."

Bennetts's book is not about rich women—not explicitly, anyway. And, to be fair, it came out before the collapse of our economy. Yet it's part of a literary genre that has long focused on a small, elite slice of American mothers as it's laid out the battle over stay-at-home motherhood versus paid work. Naomi Wolf's *Misconceptions*, Ann Crittenden's *The Price of Motherhood*, and Judith Warner's *Perfect Madness: Motherhood in the Age of Anxiety*, to name a few, also deal primarily with how upper-middle-class women encounter modern motherhood. Even Betty Friedan's *The Feminine Mystique*, which arguably launched the whole conversation about women's rightful place in the workforce in 1963, focused on highly educated professionals (or former professionals) married to successful men.

Were you a reader from another planet, you could be forgiven for assuming that at least in this neck of Earth, all moms are consumed with whether to ditch their high-powered careers or become unpaid domestic engineers–cum–pastry chefs in one of their many swank homes. You might also think women were awash in choices: to work, comfortably stay home, or any of a range of possibilities in between the two. But, in truth, only a privileged few have anything but the first option. And all too often, the "choice" of work entails a time commitment and an inflexibility that keep women away from their families more than they'd like.

This is not to say the upper crust of female earners is not important. Clearly, we have a lot to learn from the challenges and worries of high-profile professionals, whose story has been one of the central dramas of feminism. The women who fought their way into the bastions of male power, the corporate and professional worlds, were and still are fighting a pivotal battle. In even coming close to the glass ceiling and nearing professional parity, they have shown the rest of us what's possible. And to whatever extent it's happened, their exit from the highly paid workforce is an important reflection of the failure of high-level employers to accommodate their employees' caretaking responsibilities.

Yet our fixation on high-profile mothers and their employers, both real and fictional, speaks more to the problems many women wish they had than to the ones they actually do have. And by paying disproportionate attention to these uncommon dilemmas, riveting though they may be, we are siphoning off critical energy that ought to be spent addressing our all-too-real predicaments.

To be sure, there's a certain thrill in reading about the corner-office set texting their nannies on their way to meetings with clients in Hong Kong. It's like Work-Family Dilemmas of the Rich and Famous. This explains much of the appeal of Allison Pearson's page-turner novel *I Don't*

Know How She Does It.[2] The reader can't help but worry about the high-flying, fictional mom–hedge-fund manager Kate Reddy. Can she keep up her vertiginous life managing her nanny-tended family via hand-held device while maintaining her membership in the hostile men's club that is her profession? It's fun to think that such working mother-acrobats need our sympathy and exhilarating to imagine their high-wire acts. Will her client notice the formula stains on her Tahari suit? Can she find the stuffed dog and still make her plane?

We are similarly riveted by real women whose work-life dilemmas play out in the public eye: when Karen Hughes leaves the Bush White House to spend more time with her family, say, or when Caroline Kennedy retreats back into private life amid a swirl of rumors about nannies and taxes. These women are among the most prominent in recent history. Because their careers play out on the public stage, women can read their ups as inspirational legends and their downs, particularly the failure of their employers and potential employers to make room for the reality of their dual roles, as cautionary tales.

No doubt, another part of the reason we obsess about successful, high-earning mothers is that our fantasy of their lives is much more fun to ponder than the reality of ours. Even before the economy crashed around them, most women would have been lucky to have the headaches of a national politician or Pearson's fictional Reddy, who feels threatened by her kids' attachment to their nanny, is frustrated by her very patient husband, and has a high-paying, powerful job that doesn't allow her enough time for her family. Who wouldn't want to mull over her options—to continue with the aforementioned or jettison it all in exchange for a nice house in the country, more time with her children, and a small, gratifying business of her own? (Did I mention she was fictional?) It's certainly more pleasant than dwelling on the narrower and less cushy range of alternatives available to the vast majority of women.

Whatever decision Reddy makes, she's going to be better off than most women, who have neither enough money for any good, reliable child care nor satisfying work possibilities that rival the appeal of staying home with their children.

Though it's fun to dream, we focus on these fantasy problems at the expense of our real ones: the continuous struggle to find enough time and money to keep our families and work lives together—dilemmas we have to work out with *our* employers, not *theirs.* The problems we wish we had also obscure the fact that elite women already get a far better deal from their employers than everyone else does.

To the extent that the authors of the big nonfiction motherhood books have addressed class differences, they have usually argued that the predicaments of elite moms can be universalized or at least extrapolated from. In *Perfect Madness*, for instance, Warner wrote that "to understand the conflicts and, I would say, *pathologies* of upper-middle-class thinking is to understand the often perplexing state of family politics in America."[3] Writing three years after "The Opt-Out Revolution" appeared in the *Times* magazine, Belkin defends her piece as having focused explicitly on women in "the workplace stratosphere," because at other points in her career she's written about nonprofessional women.[4] For her part, Pamela Stone, the author of *Opting Out? Why Women Really Quit Careers and Head Home*, explains her narrow focus on efforts to save high-level women's jobs by arguing that the changes they bring about can "trickle down to benefit women at every level of the organization."[5]

Yet motherhood in this country clearly isn't a trickle-down proposition. And while we may identify with the problems of the highest rung of women, both due to wishful thinking and because their stories are more likely to be told, only a small fraction of women hold the kinds of professional and managerial positions that the likes of Zoe Baird, Sarah Palin, and Karen Hughes do. Women make up about 15 percent of board members and corporate officers of Fortune 500 companies, for instance.[6] And the majority of women in this professional echelon are childless.[7] The remaining few women who do manage to pull off the high-level career and motherhood combination may have the clout to command accommodations that allow them to handle their various responsibilities without getting fired, but most of us, sadly, do not.

Instead of extrapolating from the particulars of elite women's work-life situations, it makes more sense to take what you might call a "trickle-up" perspective, because the issues once associated with poor mothers are increasingly relevant to the vast majority of American women.

Focusing on the top tier can give you the sense that women are at least on their way to getting the accommodations they need from employers. Yet while women up and down the economic spectrum struggle to balance work and family, the painful truth is that the professionals who have starred in the mommy wars not only have more money to ease their double burden, they also get a bigger share of the benefits that make life livable. Women with high-paying jobs are far more likely to get flextime, paid vacations, paid maternity leave, and sick days than are women with lower-paying ones, despite the fact that lower-income workers can least afford to be docked pay or lose a job.

The unequal distribution of benefits becomes startlingly clear when you divide families into four quarters by their income level, as physician and family rights activist Jody Heymann has. Only 16 percent of families with the lowest income get more than two weeks of paid vacation and sick leave. Meanwhile, 59 percent of those with the highest income get that much time off (a figure that is still pretty anemic, when you consider that 121 countries mandate this amount of paid leave as a minimum). Perhaps more devastating for working families, fully 71 percent of the poorest working adults cannot take days off for sick children, while a far smaller proportion—34 percent—of those in the highest income bracket have the same problem, according to Heymann, the author of *The Widening Gap*.[8]

Similarly, lower-income workers who are least able to pay for child care have the least access to these benefits through an employer. Families whose income is low—yet not rock bottom, as is necessary to qualify for federal child-care assistance—have fewer good, affordable child-care options. Families living below the poverty line already spend a quarter of their income on child care, compared to the average family, which spent 6.6 percent of its income on child care, according to 2006 U.S. census numbers. Yet employer-sponsored child care, one of the most convenient possibilities for working parents, is available only to the luckiest of the lucky, who are more likely to be high-income professionals. Only 2 percent of blue-collar workers had access to employer-sponsored child care in 2006, less than the still ridiculously meager 7 percent of white-collar workers who had that benefit, according to figures from the U.S. Department of Labor.

Health coverage, too, is least available to employees on the bottom rungs of the income ladder and is becoming less, rather than more, accessible. Only 42 percent of low-wage and low-income workers have health insurance paid for in any part by their employer, while 94 percent of high-wage, high-income workers get this essential help, which can stave off medical and financial catastrophe. This inverse relationship between need and coverage, with those who can least afford to pay for care most likely to have to pay out of their own pockets, translates into millions of families' finances being destabilized by the inadequacy or the complete lack of health insurance.

Accommodations for nursing women are also more available to better-paid workers. Although not all women in powerful jobs have the privacy to nurse, they're more likely to have the flexibility and space to pump than do those further down the ladder. Women who have their own offices can shut their doors when they need to pump breast milk, for example, while their female underlings often have no private space to do the same. Even some companies that offer breast-feeding support to upper management don't necessarily extend those same benefits to lower-paid workers. The disparity was plainly apparent to Elizabeth Henschel, a textile designer who works in a Manhattan office, when she recently visited the Pennsylvania mill where the fabrics she designed are manufactured. Although she has a comfortable, private space to pump in her corporate office in Manhattan, when she asked for a place to pump at the mill, she was offered a closet with a door that didn't lock. Nursing mill workers have the same closet available to them, but all share the single space and they can use it only during their two fifteen-minute breaks during an eight-hour shift.

The inadequacy of our solutions should come as no surprise, given that they've been designed to fix our fantasy problems, rather than our real ones.

Focusing attention on the glistening tip of the iceberg and occasionally on the poorest of the poor, we've allowed ourselves to believe or at least hope that the marketplace will move employers to step up and support working parents.

But even together with government programs that are meant to help poor families, this partial solution for women at the very top does nothing for the growing number of people in between. Indeed, the most exciting workplace innovations that are often championed as the last, best hope for stressed-out mothers have little likelihood of reaching anyone not on top of the corporate ladder or off it entirely. In *Off Ramps and On Ramps*, author Sylvia Ann Hewlett writes glowingly about the flexible schedules, compressed workweeks, job sharing, part-time options, and opportunities to return after extended leaves that are available for what she calls "top talent."[9] These relatively new accommodations offered by some employers are clearly groundbreaking and necessary in the rigid corporate world that's been such a challenge for women to penetrate.

But, unfortunately, as Hewlett herself notes, such policies are also voluntary and available to only the cream of an already elite crop. The very first example of a worthy workplace accommodation noted in her book's foreword, for instance, is a possibility only for "high performing individuals" who work at American Express and who apply to and are accepted by the program. Hewlett, an economist who is also president of the Center for Work-Life Policy, a New York–based think tank, repeatedly refers to the "highly qualified women" who receive these benefits, without noting how privileged and tiny this particular lot is. Meanwhile, workers who aren't quite so talented or well-educated—or perhaps just lucky—are unlikely to reap these same accommodations.

There is indeed a good business case to be made for corporations instituting flexible workplace policies for these highly educated workers who might "opt out" without them. According to Deborah Holmes, the lawyer who spearheaded the introduction of various flexible work arrangements for the giant accounting firm Ernst & Young, these innovations, which allow both men and women to achieve better balance between work and the rest of their lives, yielded the company an extra $10 million per year. Much of the savings came from not having to find, retrain, and orient new workers to replace departing mothers, a cost that, according to Hewlett, typically runs about one-and-a-half times that person's salary.

But voluntary workplace efforts to retain women on the job after they have children, while important, are not enough even for most women in the upper echelon of jobs and certainly not for those in the middle or on the bottom of the professional ladder. Although it may be extremely worthwhile for companies to hold on to highly paid workers, keeping less-well-paid workers is less likely to be a money-saving endeavor, depending on the individual, the position, and the particulars of the company. As it is, employers have an incentive to retain their most highly trained workers only some of the time; they have fewer reasons to retain workers who cost far less to replace. Replacing a corporate attorney might run a company hundreds of thousands of dollars, for instance, while it typically costs only between $9,000 and $15,000 to replace a mid-skill-level customer service representative.[10]

As appealing as it may be to leave our problems to the marketplace, individual employers aren't likely to accommodate their workers if doing so doesn't help their bottom line, which has sunk to new lows in the current economic climate. Hewlett herself notes that men in the corporate world have hung on to the "male competitive model," which has been shaped by men who had stay-at-home wives taking care of the domestic end of things, for as long as they have because it benefits the men controlling it and disadvantages women. Programs that give a high-heeled leg up only to the corporate elite seem similarly limited, especially when they're spun as a benefit to the company's bottom line. Plus, as companies are laying off staff left and right or folding entirely, such programs are among the first casualties.

If staying home is still an alternative to hanging on to a high-end job for some women (assuming they have another high income to rely on), most women don't have the option of giving up work. For single women with children, who earn only fifty-six cents for every dollar that married men make, work is almost always necessary and yet still likely doesn't provide enough to cover costs.[11] Despite the fact that the vast majority of unmarried mothers work, they have the highest poverty rate of any demographic group.

It wasn't always this way. For many middle-class women entering the paid workforce a generation ago, work was, at first, a choice rather than a necessity and thus accommodations from employers could seem like extras. Since then, the costs of basics, such as housing and health care, have skyrocketed, wages have fallen in relation to expenses, and more work has become freelance and thus separate from health insurance. As a result, even as the average amount of money a typical two-parent family has for either discretionary spending or savings has dropped, a second income has become necessary to maintain most families' lifestyles or, in some cases, to survive.[12]

This means that many families living on one income are now struggling mightily, and that workers constrained by family needs are less likely to find accommodating work, even if they'd prefer to be employed. When Gina St. Aubin, a thirty-six-year-old mother of three in Littleton, Colorado, first got pregnant, she was happily looking forward to life as a working mom. She thoroughly enjoyed the fast pace of her full-time job as a victim's advocate, responding to crime scenes, going to court, and offering support for needy people in all sorts of situations. She and her husband had planned to have at least four children when they first met, and they figured their two salaries would provide enough to cover the basics comfortably, including regular family vacations. As she envisioned it, the clan would happily cram into the station wagon at least once a year and drive to Disney World, say, or a mountain getaway.

Seven years later, the only vacation St. Aubin and her husband have ever taken is their honeymoon. Her fantasy version of family life began to fade soon after her oldest son, Jackson, was diagnosed with cerebral palsy at nine months old. For the first few months after his diagnosis, St. Aubin continued working, but child care quickly became a pressing issue. Jackson's first sitter quit on hearing his diagnosis. A few months later, after a second babysitter admitted that she regularly left the baby by himself out of earshot when he cried, St. Aubin fired her. It soon became apparent that a qualified caretaker who was trained to work with children with Jackson's special needs would eat up most of St. Aubin's $40,000 salary. So she quit her job, in order to be able to take Jackson to his various medical and therapy appointments and, later, to care for his two younger siblings as well.

At first, staying home didn't cause much financial hardship. Without her income, the family relied entirely on the not insubstantial $80,000 her husband earns as a police sergeant to cover food, utilities, mortgage payments, and their share of medical bills. By the end of the month, St. Aubin usually wound up paying some of their bills with a credit card. But, at least for the first few years, they were able to pay back their debts with their income tax return. They even managed the occasional dinner out.

Gradually, though, their expenses began to inch up. Part of it was due to the expanding costs of their expanding family. St. Aubin gave birth to a girl when Jackson was four and a second son a year and a half after that. But the biggest financial strain was taking good care of her eldest, whose problems and costly treatments mounted as he grew. Jackson required braces on both legs, although, inexplicably, their insurance would pay only for the right one. He began to have seizures, which required additional medication. His doctor placed him on the "autism spectrum," which provided some insight into his behavioral and developmental challenges but also indicated that he needed additional therapy and medications. Because he still wasn't potty trained at age six, the family was burdened with most of the cost of his diapers, too.

Perhaps the St. Aubin family would have been able to maintain their financial stability if not for the escalating prices of everything else. As the cost of gas, groceries, clothing, and health care began to rise, Gina started to panic. She had already cut back on almost everything she could. The family dressed in secondhand clothes. They hadn't renewed their zoo pass and didn't buy birthday presents or cards. Rather than making a plate for herself at mealtime and risking the possibly of wasting food, she usually ate the children's leftovers. Jackson even stopped participating in the Special Olympics because St. Aubin felt that they couldn't afford his entry fee. Finally, she decided to cut back on her son's therapies, several of which were not covered by insurance. Although she fears that his prospects will dwindle as a result, it had come down to those out-of-pocket costs or the mortgage. St. Aubin is now thinking about looking for work but is doubtful that she'll find a job that will pay anything close to the child-care costs she'd incur or that would have the flexibility she'd need.

Facing the bleakest economy in decades, many families are grappling with similarly unimaginable choices: child care or food? Tuition or nursing home payment? Rent or medicine? The collapse of the housing market, combined with widespread job loss and the skyrocketing costs of food, gas, and other such essentials, has made the reality of many American families that much harsher and has made elite professional women's dilemmas that much less relevant.

Before the downward spiral, the depictions of extreme wealth that cropped up so often in mommy wars literature might have come off as an exercise in hopefulness. At least then, we were obsessing about a segment of the population that, albeit small, really existed. Now, after the financial free fall, the focus on elite women can seem downright delusional. Consider Sylvia Ann Hewlett's barely three-year-old description of an outreach event aimed at professional women hosted by Lehman Bros. in London, which resulted in the hiring of only four women. If there was little hope that the investment bank's program would trickle down to anyone but those four women then, there is no hope of it now, because the company, along with most investment banks, no longer exists.

Although the financial crisis is weighing heavily on everyone, in some ways women are particularly vulnerable. Already accounting for the majority of low-wage workers and poor people, women were more likely to be caught in the subprime mortgage mess and were three times more likely than men without children to go bankrupt.[13] Indeed, in this changed economy, the increasingly irrelevant question of whether women ought to work or stay home is being replaced with the far more dramatic challenge of basic survival. If they can get a job these days, most women have no choice but to take it.

Even then, for a startling number of families, work doesn't ensure a decent life. In 2006, well before the mortgage crisis, the credit collapse, and the subsequent nationwide belt-tightening, about a quarter of workers earned $10 or less per hour.[14] An additional 20 percent earned less than $25,000 per year. Together, these low-wage workers make up almost half of the workforce and, because they are more likely to have children (more than 80 percent of lower-income families have children, as opposed to less than two-thirds of other families), low-income mothers and fathers account for more than half of working parents.[15]

An even greater percentage of families and children, while not meeting the country's strict (many would say outdated) definition of poverty, are actually hanging by a financial thread. At least one-quarter of all jobs in the United States paid less than $9.38 an hour in 2006, which is what a family of four needed to earn to climb above the poverty level, according to the Center for Law and Social Policy.[16] Even though the federal minimum wage was given a much-needed increase in 2007, it's still impossible for a family to live comfortably on such low pay. At just $7.25 per hour, up from $5.15 per hour, where it had remained since 1997, a forty-hour workweek still grosses an income of $15,080 per year. It's almost impossibly difficult to support a family; rent, buy, or maintain a home; or purchase health insurance on that money, let alone pay for children's higher education or plan for retirement.

Clearly, the ability to provide the basics is slipping away from many families. The number of children going hungry rose by 50 percent in 2007 and continues to climb.[17] The number of homeless families has exploded, with 459 school districts reporting an increase of at least 25 percent in the number of homeless students identified between the 2007–2008 school year and the previous school year.[18]

While most middle-income families could once count on financial stability and the ability to at least feed and clothe their offspring in exchange for their work, they are increasingly vulnerable to job loss, bankruptcy, eviction, and foreclosure that used to haunt only those on the very lowest rung of our economy. Even the best-educated and highest of fliers cannot assume they'll consistently receive decent pay and benefits. (Witness the plague of underemployment that's been visited on former Wall Streeters.) Many working women with college and even graduate degrees find themselves slamming into the outdated expectation that working hard and staying in school will somehow guarantee stability.

Yet as we've dwelt on the work-life dilemmas of the upper echelon, these other stories have been overlooked. When an early version of this chapter made this point on the Web site Salon.com, many readers responded with stories of their own seemingly invisible struggles. As one woman who works part-time as an adjunct professor at a community college and splits child care with her husband wrote in her post, "A quick glance at our parenting decisions and work habits may seem to yield the assumption that we are well-off and have the luxury of staying at home. Yet the reality is that we are almost poor, sometimes choose between food and paying the rent, and often come face-to-face with despair. We make the best of a hopelessly insufficient situation."

Meanwhile, many other women—the women who were poor well before the downturn—are even worse off. And perhaps because their ongoing struggles are not new, they get even less public attention.[19] Unable to either opt out or rely on employers to make life livable, many women, especially lower-paid ones, are caught in an agonizing bind. Less likely to have flexibility, advancement opportunities, or even predictable schedules, their job situations are that much more difficult to escape. After more than a decade of low-paying work, Forleta Jenkins, a twenty-eight-year-old mother of three living in Hollandale, Mississippi, has all but stopped trying.

Hollandale, a small town in the notoriously depressed Delta region, has few residents (2,991 when I was there in 2007) and even fewer jobs. One of the biggest employers is the catfish-processing plant run by Consolidated Catfish in nearby Isola, Mississippi, where Jenkins has worked trimming fish for the last seven years. But despite her tenure, she has irregular hours and little control over their scheduling. During the "off-flavor" season, which includes the spring and the summer, the fish give off a mysterious earthy odor that makes them less appealing to eaters, and workers at the plant typically have fewer hours than they'd like. In May, when I met Jenkins, for instance, she had worked only twenty-three hours the previous week and estimated that she would make only $700 in total wages by the end of the month, barely enough to pay her bills.

During the winter, when the catfish are more reliably tasty, Jenkins and her coworkers often put in shifts of more than twelve hours. The busy season is a mixed blessing, though. She has to find someone else to pick up her children from child care during those months, and she has little time to spend with them or do anything else after she gets home. But Forleta Jenkins stays in the job because she can't find anything better. And, presumably, her employer doesn't offer her more flexibility or predictability because it doesn't have to.

There is, of course, a vast gap between Jenkins, who nervously awaits her weekly schedule in the catfish plant every week, and Wendy Greenberg, of luxury holiday cookie fame. The two live on opposite sides of a great divide within our country. The average per capita income in Hollandale of $11,293 per year is less than a fifth of the average income in the toniest Manhattan zip code and is low even for

Mississippi, the poorest state in the nation. The vast majority of women fall somewhere in between these two extremes. The problem is that while we have come to think of ourselves as a nation of Wendy Greenbergs, most of us now actually have far more in common with Forleta Jenkins.

5

Testing the Bootstraps

What Exactly Is Keeping the Women of Mississippi Down?

Less than a mile from the capitol building in Jackson, Mississippi, a handful of people gather outside an unassuming stucco building on North State Street. If not for their "I'll Pray for You" and "Don't Kill Your Baby" signs, which sit propped up against a car as often as they're held in the air, you could miss the fact that these are protesters, and that this small, pale-pink building that they mill about in front of is an abortion clinic. Indeed, the Jackson Women's Health Organization is not merely an abortion clinic; it's the only remaining abortion clinic in the entire state. There used to be others. In 1996, there were six medical facilities that provided abortions in Mississippi. But since August 2004, there has been only this one in Jackson. Although the clinic was staffed by three part-time physicians as recently as five years ago, only one doctor remains today.

Once you make it past the protestors, the interior of the modest waiting room might surprise you, too. Not the tasteful prints on the walls, the dated magazines, or even the somewhat battered mauve vinyl chairs, but the fact that on most days, quite a few of those chairs are empty. Usually, three or four are filled by young women, not infrequently wearing loose clothing and preoccupied expressions. Still, the clinic is strikingly not a bustling place, especially considering the lack of competition. On each of several occasions I visited, there were always empty chairs.

A small, mostly rural population and the absence of local pro-choice organizations has helped turn Mississippi into the perfect test ground for antiabortion strategists. Virtually every possible restriction on the procedure exists here, from a mandatory twenty-four-hour waiting period after counseling to a requirement that minors obtain the consent of both parents to have an abortion, to thirty-five pages of regulations dealing with such physical characteristics as the width of a clinic's hallways and the size of its parking lot. Unfortunately, Mississippi's apparent concern for unborn babies doesn't translate into concern for already existing children. It's an oft discussed irony about the pro-life movement. Still, the state's extremes are striking. Accompanying its near ban on abortion, Mississippi has the second-highest rate of child poverty in the country. (Only Washington D.C.'s is higher.)[1]

Yet the real irony goes deeper than that: the state with arguably the least access to reproductive services, including abortion, is also the state with the worst infant mortality rate. For every 1,000 live births, 10.1 infants under age one died in Mississippi in 2007, a rate that's gone up in recent years, even as the rest of the country's has gone down. In parts of the impoverished Delta region, the number of deaths exceeds 20.[2] (The national infant mortality rate, by comparison, is 6.7.)[3]

I came to Mississippi to figure out what exactly is dragging women like Forleta Jenkins, the mother who works in the catfish plant, down into poverty and keeping them there. The State Street protestors and the people who agree with their politics, often thought of as proponents of "family values," would probably tell you it's a lack of personal responsibility. If poor women worked harder and cleaned up their acts, their lives wouldn't be so hard. But my travels in Mississippi cemented my conviction that the lack of control over the decision to have children and the dearth of support for them afterward is nearer the heart of the problem. Despite the term's antiabortion implications, "family values" in their truest sense would include these basics. Without them, I was reminded as I traveled throughout the state, it's all but impossible for women and their children to do well.

Clearly, the "magnolia state," with its sweet-smelling flowered trees, decaying slavery-era plantations, and sky-high unemployment rates, is a place of extremes. If, as we've been told, there are two Americas, Mississippi is way on the red, religious, and poor side of the divide. The only state that issues both "God Bless America" and "Choose Life" license plates, Mississippi has more churches per capita than any other state, with almost half of its residents identifying as Evangelical Protestants. It's also among the reddest of red states politically, having cast its six electoral votes for the Republican presidential candidate in every election since 1976. Mississippi holds another distinction: with women here more likely to be poor than in any other state, it's the women's poverty capital of the country. Indeed, Mississippi is, overall, the very poorest state in the entire nation. Because of its extremity, by my trickle-up theory, Mississippi could lend insight not only into the troubles facing poor women throughout the country, but into those plaguing women further up the economic spectrum.

But how were these extremes—the state's resistance to abortion and its sky-high women's poverty rate—connected? For their part, the abortion restrictions have been largely successful, in that many of those waiting room chairs remain empty. While there were 19.4 abortions for every thousand women of reproductive age nationwide in 2005, in Mississippi there were fewer than 5, down from more than 13 in 1991. But figuring out how the tenuousness of women's control over reproduction contributes to women's poverty was complicated by the fact that the relationship also works in reverse: lack of money cuts into Mississippi women's ability to decide when and if to have children. Many poor women can't even get birth control here. Only about two in five women and teens in Mississippi who need publicly financed contraception receive it, according to the most recent figures from the Alan Guttmacher Institute, which does research on reproductive issues. Although the inability to prevent unwanted pregnancies makes women only more likely to want abortions, many of the forces behind the strong antiabortion movement here also oppose contraception. The advocacy group Pro-Life Mississippi, for instance, is waging a campaign against both "morning after" pills and birth control pills.

Of course, anyone who can't pay twenty-something dollars a month for a pack of pills is even less likely to have the more than $400 it costs for an abortion. Betty Thompson hears from these girls and women daily. Thompson, who worked as a counselor at the Jackson Women's Health Organization for years, then became its director, and is now a consultant to the clinic, says women often call saying they want abortions but don't have the money to pay for them. A stately grandmother who had her first child at age sixteen, Thompson always encourages resourcefulness in the women she counsels who are struggling to pay for abortions. "I ask them, 'Have you sold your jewelry yet? Have you asked to borrow from everyone you know?'" As Thompson is aware, the stakes in the money scramble are high, because too much dallying can easily push women further into their pregnancies.

Research backs Thompson's anecdotal evidence that a lack of money can cause women to delay having abortions, making them more difficult, more expensive, and sometimes out of reach altogether. Sixty-seven percent of poor women having an abortion say they would have preferred to have had it earlier, according to a 2004 study.[4] Specifically, researchers have determined that poor women take additional time in confirming a pregnancy, as well as several more days between making the decision to have an abortion and actually obtaining one. In Mississippi, where only one of fifty counties has an abortion provider, the logistics of getting the procedure can be particularly daunting: First there is the long drive to Jackson, then the phalanx of protesters surrounding the clinic, followed by the two-day ordeal that begins with the informational session and ends, finally—at least twenty-four hours after that session—with the abortion.

Some particularly desperate women may even resort to illegal abortions. In the Delta, the poorest region in the state, parts of which are four hours from Mississippi's one clinic, "lay midwives" minister to unwanted pregnancies, according to several sources. Other women get around the obstacles by traveling. Because of the intensely hostile climate toward abortion, between one-quarter and one-third of Mississippi women went out of state to end their pregnancies, according to researchers who studied the state in 2000.[5] But the trip to Louisiana or Tennessee or Alabama requires time off from work, a car, and gas money—hurdles that, especially for poor women, are sometimes insuperable.

Consider Tammy, a mom who first came into the Jackson clinic in her fourteenth week of pregnancy. Because that put her past the state's legal limit for an abortion, she was told she'd have to make a trip to Alabama. Since she's single, she would have had to arrange for overnight child care for her trip, because that state, too, has a twenty-four-hour waiting limit. She struggled mightily to raise the money to go, according to Cheryl McGee, a staff member at Jackson Women's Health Organization, but didn't manage to do it in time. "She had just started her job and she couldn't get no time off and she couldn't get nobody to take her," explains McGee. "She doesn't have a car to get there, and she didn't have the money to get a bus."

It's hard to imagine someone who can't afford a bus trip taking responsibility for a new life—especially when she doesn't want to. Yet Tammy went on to have and keep her baby some six months later. This, no doubt, is the outcome that the pro-life movement hoped for in erecting Mississippi's various obstacles to abortion: a new life. Yet this "success" brings us to the other part of the story begged by the empty seats in the clinic waiting room: how poor women like Tammy can lose ground once their pregnancies go on to become people.

Another eerily empty office on North State Street helps explain part of the process. Housed in a boxy black-and-white building, the Mississippi Department of Human Services is the heart of the bureaucracy that Tammy and other struggling mothers might turn to were they to seek help with housing, food, or subsistence. Yet it wouldn't necessarily provide them with what they need. According to the department's official mission statement, that branch of state government aims to "encourage traditional family values," which promote "self-sufficiency and personal responsibility for all Mississippians." In other words, at least in terms of spending on women and children, less is more.

According to the dominant theory of social services that first sprouted when Reagan came to office in 1980 and came into full bloom with the Clinton-era overhaul of welfare in 1996, low levels of public support can nudge low-income women into taking greater responsibility for themselves and their families (and thus become less of a burden on other taxpayers). While the entire country has, to varying degrees, adopted this framework and accordingly cut back on publicly funded social programs, Mississippi has distinguished itself in this realm, too, by granting record low levels of aid to support women with children. True to its mission, Mississippi's Department of Human Services offers rock-bottom funding for child-care assistance, cash welfare benefits, foster-care programs, food stamps, Medicaid, Head Start, and child health insurance, making it perhaps the best place in the country to gauge the success of our country's sink-or-swim approach to poverty.

Although Mississippi may be the worst offender, it's not alone in treating mothers poorly. More than 15 percent of women with children nationwide lived in households with "low or very low food security" in 2006.[6] Mothers are also particularly vulnerable in terms of housing, with families—overwhelmingly headed by single women—making up the fastest-growing group of the homeless population. Eighteen percent of mothers nationwide lacked health insurance in 2007 (as opposed to 16 percent of fathers), while in Mississippi, fully 26 percent of mothers were uninsured, according to the Center on Budget and Policy Priorities.[7]

The correlation between having laws that don't support reproductive choice, as well as those that fail to help mothers and children, noted by Jean Reith Schroedel in "Is the Fetus a Person?" should not be entirely surprising.[8] A political scientist who focused on banking policy before she began to track public interest in protecting fetuses, Schroedel looked state by state at policies and found that concern about protecting the unborn lined up with antiabortion values, rather than with concern or services for existing children. She also found that women in antiabortion states are generally worse off than their counterparts in pro-choice states, suffering from lower levels of education, less mandated insurance coverage for minimum hospital stays after childbirth, higher levels of poverty, and a larger gender gap in earnings.

One explanation for this phenomenon is that states with low budgets tend to spend less on everything from services for women to office supplies. Mississippi, with a relatively small tax base and overall budget, clearly fits that mold. But the conservative thinking that drives the restrictions on both abortion and social spending is another big reason for the connection.

In this mind-set, spending on abortion, sex education, birth control, and even services for low-income single mothers is seen as encouraging promiscuity.

At least in terms of promiscuity, the verdict is in. With Mississippi having the highest rate of teen pregnancy in the nation and very high rates of births overall and single motherhood in particular, the strategy of cutting back on services is clearly failing to deter people from having sex. Whether those teens and other moms who didn't necessarily intend to get pregnant wind up being especially independent or self-reliant, as the bootstraps strategists would predict, is a separate question. To answer it, I decide to head north from the slow and steamy city of Jackson and drive to the even slower and steamier Delta region, which has high birth and poverty rates even for Mississippi.

Although it may seem crass to reduce human life to numbers—fertility rates, sizes of families, the timing of children, and dollars and cents—for many mothers, pregnancy, birth, and all that follows in raising a child often amount to a huge and measurable setback. The same, it should be noted, is not true for men—or at least not to the same extent. While many couples share the responsibilities and burdens of parenthood, the costs are typically not distributed equally. There are very few studies that attempt to measure the financial impact of children on men's earnings (a significant fact, in and of itself), but the few that do attempt this find that men do not typically pay a monetary price as a result of their fatherhood. In fact, having children was correlated with higher salaries for men, even as it was correlated with lower salaries for women, in one 1999 study of 829 male and female MBAs published in *Sex Roles*.[9]

In contrast, becoming a mother before finishing school, whether high school or college, can tip the balance, pushing a young woman into poverty, a state from which it's certainly more difficult to emerge while being responsible for children.

For those who are already poor, a child can push them deeper into poverty for a longer time. Although much national attention has focused on the cost of teen pregnancy in terms of lost income and opportunities, there is little recognition that many of these costs remain well after a woman reaches her twenties, a socially acceptable age for parenting and yet still a time of life when most people who will establish satisfying careers are continuing their education and training. Even though a twenty-year-old woman wouldn't be considered a teen mother if she had a child, for instance, she still wouldn't have reached the age at which she could finish college and be eligible for most well-paying jobs.

In her 2001 book *The Price of Motherhood*, Ann Crittenden calculated that the typical college-educated woman in America loses roughly $1 million in a lifetime after having one child, a figure that includes the earnings and the social security she forgoes during the time she spends at home caring for the child.[10] The actual dollar amount for women who don't have college degrees would be lower, if you figure that they'd likely earn lower wages and would probably spend less feeding, clothing, housing, and schooling children, because the wealthier the parents, typically, the more they spend on their children. (The average family making $76,520 or more will spend $252,300 to raise a child, according to a 2008 Department of Agriculture survey, while those earning below $36,330 will spend $189,690.)[11]

But the price of motherhood might be just as high or higher for low-income women, if you include the cost of deferred and delayed education borne by those who didn't start or complete school as a result of having children. Take Forleta

Jenkins again, the single mother who works at the catfish plant in Hollandale, Mississippi. Jenkins, who had her first child, unplanned, after graduating from high school, says she had intended to go to college to study elementary education and ultimately work in that field. But more than ten years after that first pregnancy, she still hasn't found a way to go to school while taking care of her children and working. She lives close to the edge, raising three children on the $7.80 per hour she earns trimming catfish in the nearby town of Isola, and fears that asking her employer for time off to go to school would jeopardize her job and the modicum of stability she's achieved in her seven years at the plant. (When a spokesman for Consolidated Catfish was asked about allowing employees to work around their school schedules, he said the company might be open to such an arrangement, but that no employees have yet requested it.) Meanwhile, Jenkins has been in a holding pattern, scraping by on her meager earnings and longing for a career that remains a distant dream.

It's impossible to know whether, in fact, Jenkins would have become a teacher if she hadn't gotten pregnant when she did, and what exactly her financial situation would now be. But the average salary for a classroom teacher in Mississippi was $41,215 in the 2008 to 2009 school year, according to the state's department of education, which is about $26,215 per year more than Jenkins says she earned that year at the catfish plant.[12] After more than ten years at the plant, with her third child now six years old, she is earning a little more than $15,000 a year, by her estimate. Even if she were to return to school next year at age twenty-nine (something she says she'd like to do but isn't confident she can pull off), the timing of her motherhood in combination with the lack of job flexibility has already cost her more than $262,150—and that figure doesn't account for the better benefits that would come from the teaching job or the greater social security income she would accrue after holding the higher-paid teaching position.

Although their numbers are just approximations, a few economists have done their best to quantify the price that women really pay for having children. According to Leonard M. Lopoo, a public policy scholar at Syracuse University, a number of factors increase women's chances of living in poverty, all of which, it happens, apply to Forleta Jenkins, a single African American woman who had her children early and has no college education.[13] Lopoo notes that women in the South, in particular, tend to be poorer, in part because they usually have less education and have their children at earlier ages. Both factors compound the chances that a mother will live in poverty, as does race, with non-Hispanic white women having the lowest poverty rates. By Lopoo's calculation, each child a woman has on average increases her probability of being poor by 5.4 percentage points.

Of course, no mother looks at her child, whether planned or not, and sees a 5.4 percentage-point curse. But the experience of falling into motherhood before becoming financially established, rather than choosing it, clearly colors a woman's feelings about the experience.

The last observation comes to mind when I meet Shaneika, a twenty-five-year-old single mother who, like Jenkins, lives in Hollandale, Mississippi. A small cross-hatch of streets a few miles east of the Mississippi River, the town of Hollandale emerges from the surrounding farmland suddenly and, after a few blocks lined with trees and the occasional one-story house, gives way again to still, green fields just as suddenly. I met Shaneika at the World of Love Early Childhood Academy, located at one of Hollandale's main intersections—okay, one of its only intersections. We talked there over the din of children, including Shaneika's, playing and laughing in the next room. A muscular woman with slicked-back hair and a sense of humor, Shaneika doesn't hesitate when I ask what she thinks her life would have been like if she hadn't had her two unplanned children, then six months and six years old. "Perfect," she answers without missing a beat.

The laugh and sigh that follow her answer hint at more complicated feelings. Clearly, she has affection for her children, whom she admits to missing while she's at work as a cashier at a gas station. And in her fantasy life, she says, she'd be able to afford to stay home with them a few days a week and take them on a vacation (it would be the family's first). But for now, that dream remains just that, because it's all but impossible to care for her children while making her way toward attaining a college degree, a better job, and, ultimately, financial stability.

After two years of working steadily at the Quik-Mart, Shaneika, who asked to go by just her first name, still makes an hourly wage of only $5.80. Her hours are unpredictable: on Mondays, she looks at the schedule to see when she'll have to work. All too often, it's the 3 p.m. to midnight shift, which means she won't get to see her kids in the evenings. And she has no immediate hope for a raise or better employment. Like Forleta Jenkins, since dropping out of college after having a child at nineteen, she has been unable to arrange for child care so she can attend school at night.

Shaneika dreams of returning to college to get an undergraduate degree in social work soon (her hope is that her boyfriend will stay with the children at night), but she worries about the strain it will place on her family.

Lashonda Turner, a twenty-eight-year-old single mom in the same town, could tell Shaneika that her fears are well-founded. Although all of the single mothers I interviewed in Hollandale said they wanted to go back to school, Turner was alone in having managed to resume her education while her children were young. Halfway through her undergraduate degree, she studies and goes to classes at night after spending her days earning just $6 an hour for her full-time child-care work at A World of Love.

Turner is lucky, in that her younger sister can now take care of her three children—ages twelve, five, and four—at night, feeding them and putting them to bed, before Turner herself gets back from school around nine thirty. The rest of her evening usually entails checking her eldest son's homework, eating, and cleaning up the house before falling into bed around eleven thirty, which allows her just six hours of sleep before having to wake up the next day and start all over again. Grueling as it may be, Turner knows she will probably look back on this as "the easy part," because her sister will start college at night in the fall, leaving Turner in a child-care bind. One way or another, she's hopeful that she'll eventually get her degree so she can get a better job and someday be around to help her son with his homework while he's awake. She hopes then to have more energy and time to play with her children. These days, she spends her rare spare moments sleeping.

There is no question that Turner, Jenkins, and Shaneika are remarkably independent and self-reliant people, managing work and caring for their children with little help and money. But ask Turner whether she's living the life she wants or even thriving and the answer will be a roll of the eyes and a sigh that let you know just how far she feels from success. Broader measures echo Turner's judgment that the state's poor women have decidedly not lifted themselves up by their bootstraps. According to the census, almost 25 percent of women in Mississippi live in poverty, as opposed to slightly less than 15 percent nationwide.[14] Meanwhile, the state regularly ranks dead last on various measures of well-being, as it did in the most recent National Women's Law Center's report on women's health and the Institute for Women's Policy Research's most recent report on women's overall status.[15] And with the teen pregnancy rate and the overall birth rate climbing, the immediate future only looks worse.

In part, the bootstraps approach seems to fail because, like the "supermom" myth, it's underpinned by the assumption that the success of low-income working mothers is a simple matter of effort. But it's hard to imagine Lashonda Turner sleeping any less or, for that matter, any of the women I spoke with in Hollandale working any harder than they do. Instead, their difficulties stem from the near impossibility of attaining the education they need to get decent jobs, while at the same time shouldering the demands of motherhood, often on their own. If they don't succeed, it's because, without the power to delay motherhood or the ability to obtain more help after it arrives, the deck is stacked against them.

Some women, though, are immune to the specific problems plaguing the poor women of Mississippi. Just as an unexpected child can bring financial ruin, financial stability—and the work necessary to attain and maintain it—can easily slide into women never having children. Fully one in five American women between forty and forty-four was childless in 2007, according to census figures, twice the rate recorded thirty years before that. In general, the higher a woman's income, the less likely she is to have children. Nearly half of women with annual incomes over $100,000 had no children, according to the 2001 survey that Sylvia Ann Hewlett incorporated into her book *Creating a Life*.

As Lashonda Turner can tell you, the process of determining one's reproductive fate is more complicated than simply having access to birth control or an abortion provider. Like all of the other women I spoke with in Hollandale, Turner, who had her first child at sixteen, did choose not to get an abortion, but she didn't choose to get pregnant in the first place. Due to some combination of ignorance and wishful thinking, about half of sexually active people in their twenties dwell in this gray area, not wanting to get pregnant, yet still not using birth control either consistently or at all. As a result, nearly 10 percent of all unmarried women younger than thirty get pregnant unexpectedly each year. Among single women in their twenties, fully seven in ten pregnancies are unplanned, according to a 2009 study by the National Campaign to Prevent Teen and Unplanned Pregnancy.

As it does for most young women, Turner's unplanned pregnancy set her on a course that, had she alternatives, she likely wouldn't have picked.

Money, of course, expands women's options, giving them access not only to birth control and abortion, but also to fertility treatments that can help them conceive later in life. Still, the phenomenon of childlessness among many high-income women, which has largely been viewed as a matter of choice, is, like the phenomenon of early, unplanned childbearing, more complicated than that. Clearly, some of the booming numbers of women who don't have children truly don't want to. As the social pressure on women to procreate has eased somewhat, they've made clear-cut, conscious decisions to fill their lives with other things. In 2002, some 10.3 percent of women between forty and forty-four were voluntarily childless—or childfree, as some prefer—up from 2.3 percent in 1982.[16] For some others, though, the decision process is murkier, and they wind up without children less by design than because they can't find a way to fit them into their lives. With good reason, many of these higher-income women clearly fear that having a child will mean sacrificing all they've achieved in the workplace. (The top two reasons women gave for putting off pregnancy, according to a 2005 study published in *Fertility and Sterility*, were that they were "not financially ready" and "wanted to establish career.")[17]

Whatever their decision, educated women often have a complicated calculus around the question of having children that seems to defy our favored catchall term of the moment, "reproductive choice."

Although their dilemmas may seem dissimilar, at root, low-income women who find themselves with limited professional options after having children early are actually grappling with the same difficulty that high-income women are: simultaneously managing both paid work and child-raising. Because building a career and raising children tend to happen around the same time in a woman's life, without enough support, one or the other tends to win out. Thus, just as career women sometimes find themselves having drifted past the point of being able to get pregnant, low-income women snowed under by the pressures of parenting, without enough income and flexibility to get further education, can find themselves unable get beyond their low-paying and unsatisfying jobs. And without an escape hatch, a poverty spell brought on by an untimely birth becomes a life in poverty.

6

Congratulations, Now Back to Work

Keeping Mothers and Babies Apart

From its name, you'd think the Mesa Grand Family Community would be a happy, buzzing place, maybe a little like Mr. Rogers's neighborhood or the kids' corner at a county fair. But when you find it—if you find it—the trailer park looks more like it's on the moon. If you accidentally pass the entrance on an unmarked road in an unnamed area just north of Las Cruces, New Mexico, you'll notice that the pavement quickly gives way to paprika-like dust. Scan the horizon for signs of family or community, and instead you'll see that the desolate red surface seems to extend forever. Eventually, perhaps because it's the only thing around, you may stumble on Mesa Grand's few rows of lonely-looking trailers. No children swing on the park's monkey bars. No one strolls between the homes. Only the low hum of air conditioners suggests the existence of actual inhabitants.

But step into the trailer at space #73, the Lopez family's double-wide, and the post-apocalyptic feeling quickly falls away. Student-of-the-month certificates and football and baseball awards plaster the walls. Baby noises fill the air. In the living room, bright baby toys are arranged in a semicircle. Within it, Kalen Lopez and her four-month-old daughter, Carissa, do their best Madonna-and-child impersonation. Dressed in a lavender onesie, Carissa sits on Kalen's knee, gazing up placidly at her mother, a serene woman with porcelain skin and long brown hair twisted into an old-fashioned bun. If someone could translate the tiny girl's gurgles, they'd probably learn that she was proclaiming her family's vitality. "Never mind the moonscape trailer park," she might be cooing. "The Lopez clan is decidedly not heading into oblivion."

During our many conversations, Kalen Lopez often has at least one hand on her daughter, smoothing down some of her fine black hair or stroking the girl's cheek. On this warm October morning, she jiggles Carissa on her knee while talking about her first experience of stay-at-home motherhood. Our conversation travels a path well worn by new mothers, from nap schedule to nursing issues, and eventually settles on the little girl's quickly improving nighttime sleep. Lopez can lovingly describe the content of her daughter's diaper like the most wide-eyed of first-time moms, although, in fact, the smiley Carissa is her third child. Cupping one of her daughter's small feet in her palm, she reflects on the different sorts of experiences she had when her sons, Paul Jr., ten, and Patrick, six, were infants.

Motherhood wasn't nearly as enjoyable the first two times around. When her oldest was this age, Kalen was sixteen and preparing to return to work full-time as a customer service representative at the local phone company. High school was already a memory. Unexpectedly pregnant, she had dropped out in her junior year, moved in with Paul, then her boyfriend, and set about earning her way in the world. (Lopez married Paul when Junior was one and earned her high school equivalency diploma three years later.)

Four years later, when she had Patrick, Lopez had to return to her job at the phone company only three weeks after giving birth. She had desperately wanted to nurse Patrick, and her doctor strongly advised it because her older son, who was formula-fed for most of his infancy, had developed asthma and allergies. But her milk dried up shortly after she returned to work. "Pumping was just so hard. I had to do it in a restroom stall, and there was no freezer [to store the breast milk]," Lopez recalls now, as she rubs Carissa's back. "I felt like I had failed." Indeed, like his brother, Patrick wound up developing asthma and allergies, ailments that breast-feeding has been shown to help prevent. In Patrick's case, the respiratory problems were complicated by a respiratory syncytial virus infection that required hospitalization and prevented him from attending group day care.

Lopez wasn't doing so well herself at the time. Working ten hours a day during the week, in addition to half-day shifts every other Saturday and caring for her two children in her "spare" time, she was exhausted. At $5.15 an hour with no benefits, her job scarcely seemed worth the hardship. But Paul wasn't earning enough as a janitor in a local public school to support the family. His bi-weekly paycheck was just $411, which was barely enough to cover day-care costs. Even with their combined incomes, Lopez sometimes had to borrow money to pay for diapers or gas to get to work.

This time around, Lopez has beaten the dismal postpartum odds, having won the equivalent of the maternity-leave jackpot. Because the family's income is still below poverty level, she qualifies not only for Temporary Assistance for Needy Families, or TANF, the current incarnation of welfare, but also for a small pilot program that allows her to stay home with Carissa for the first year of the child's life. To Lopez's ongoing amazement, New Mexico's small policy experiment known as at-home infant care, or AHIC, provides her with $250 per month and, more important, a full year off work to be with her baby. In contrast to TANF, which supplies Lopez with an additional $568 per month and would otherwise require her to work, the pilot program stipulates that Lopez not hold a job or attend school during the year she gets its support.

For the first time in her ten years of motherhood, she can spend a significant amount of time with her infant before going back to work. Although she has to attend a weekly parenting class, her time is otherwise her own, an arrangement that Lopez says leaves her feeling "really, really lucky."

With only twelve parents enrolled in the Las Cruces pilot program and another handful taking part in a similar program in Bernalillo, a small town north of Albuquerque, New Mexico's program is tiny. Yet as small as it is, the policy experiment gets at, if it can't really resolve, a little-addressed problem that is so huge, a majority of American mothers become its casualties. Although staying home with one's own very young children is lauded as noble, most people can't afford to do it. Despite the fact that many people think the problem of maternity leave was resolved with the Family and Medical Leave Act, most parents don't get to stay home with their newborns for anywhere close to the twelve-week maximum leave allowed by the legislation.

Such a brutal launch into parenthood sets the hostile stage for working mothers from their children's infancies onward. It sometimes derails careers and often causes both women and their young children to suffer. Yet, whether living in poverty or not, for too many women, mothering an infant is closer to the experience Lopez had the first two times—something done in utter exhaustion during the small snatches between shifts—than the laid-back love affair she is now enjoying with Carissa. Although a majority of mothers want to work outside the house when their children are older and some are ready to go back to their jobs fairly soon after giving birth, many working women want more time at home with their little ones than they get. Indeed, spending any significant amount of time with babies even in their first months of life has come to be a relatively rare privilege. Only 42 percent of working women in the United States stay home for the entire first twelve weeks of their infants' lives.[1] Instead, the majority return to work before that three-month mark—often before their children have cracked their first tiny smiles.

In its extremity, the problem is uniquely American. And, in its uniquely American way, the routine prying of mothers from their small babies has been met with a commercial, rather than an appropriate governmental, response. To the aid of addled, sleep-deprived, and perhaps grief-stricken mothers comes an array of educational toys, developmental aids, and infant formula specifically enhanced for brain growth. Yet if classical musical CDs for babies fill a need, perhaps it's not only "to instill a lifelong love of music," as the

Baby Einstein Web site suggests, but also to assuage the guilt and sadness their mothers feel at not having enough time to spend with their young children.

Women in the United States aren't guaranteed any paid maternity leave, making it the only industrialized country and one of only five nations—rich or poor—not to grant new mothers paid time off.[2] The Family and Medical Leave Act, passed under Clinton in 1993, guarantees new parents up to twelve weeks off after a birth or an adoption. But slightly more than half of workers are able to take advantage of it. Parents who work for small companies or are self-employed, are unemployed, or have recently changed jobs are out of luck. Devorah Gartner, for instance, didn't qualify because she hadn't been directly employed by her company for an entire year when she needed the time off. With all of FMLA's restrictions, higher-paid employees are more likely to be covered by the law than are lower-paid ones. Only 39 percent of workers making less than $20,000 per year were covered by the law, for instance, as opposed to 74 percent of those earning more than $100,000.[3]

Even if they do qualify for our nation's meager leave policy, families eking by on low wages are often unable to afford to take advantage of it. A substantial minority of those entitled to unpaid leave couldn't take it, according to the best study to date. In the eighteen months leading up to a 2000 survey on use of the FMLA commissioned by the Department of Labor, some 2.73 million workers eligible for leave under the FMLA didn't take it because they couldn't afford it.[4]

Because providing paid maternity or paternity leave is left up to the discretion of employers, it's become a sort of luxury, something available only with plum jobs at "family-friendly" companies. Yet even the best workplaces aren't very generous with the amount of paid leave they offer new mothers and fathers. Take the top hundred employers chosen by *Working Mother* magazine in 2006, which every year honors certain companies for the sensitivity of their policies that affect female employees. These are the shining exemplars of American employment policy, yet more than half provided only six weeks or less of paid parental leave, according to an analysis done by the Institute for Women's Policy Research.[5] When you consider employers who are not the crème de la crème, the picture gets far worse. Among all private-sector employees, only 8 percent have any paid leave at all.[6]

Not surprisingly, the lack of paid leave creates the biggest problems for the lowest-paid workers, such as Lopez, who are already overrepresented among new parents. Poverty rates are highest and low-income jobs most common among the parents of young children, because they tend to be younger and have less work experience. Yet low-paid workers generally have the flimsiest benefits: a mere 5 percent of workers making less than $15 an hour have paid leave, as opposed to 11 percent of those making more than that wage.[7] And the number of women getting paid maternity leave is now headed down, rather than up. In 2008, just 16 percent of employees were offered fully paid, six-week maternity leaves, as opposed to 27 percent a decade ago, according to a study by the Families and Work Institute, a nonprofit research center based in New York.[8] Without the paid leave or the financial cushion to take a full twelve weeks of unpaid leave, many new mothers wind up going back to work well before they feel ready to.

Through a variety of policies, including extended maternity, paternity, and parental leave, many other countries make it possible for parents to be with their young infants and young children for extended periods without becoming destitute or unemployed. Both France and Spain provide about six years of leave for a couple, in which a parent can hold on to a job while staying home with a child. Germany, Austria, and Norway similarly protect parents' jobs for between two and three years, while also providing paid leave for forty-two to forty-seven weeks after a birth. Sweden offers one of the most drool-worthy examples. A woman there is allowed to ultimately return to her job even if she continues to stay home until her child is a year and a half (a benefit that would no doubt have appealed to Devorah Gartner). Then, until that child is eight years old, parents, whether male or female, are entitled to work six-hour days at prorated pay.

But it's not only Northern European or even wealthy nations that make us look bad. American maternity benefits are downright paltry compared with those of just about any other nation. Ninety-eight countries not only offer workers more than fourteen weeks off, with the right to return to a job; they make sure that leave is paid, according to a recent study of 177 countries representing a wide range of economic and political systems conducted by Jody Heymann of McGill University's Institute for Health and Social Policy and the Global Institute on Working Families.[9] One hundred and sixty-eight countries, including Djibouti, a small drought-plagued nation in Africa, offer some form of paid time off to women who have just given birth.

Poorer countries also do far better by their families than the United States does. Consider, for instance, maternity leave policies in South America. Bolivia, the poorest country on its continent, grants women three months of fully paid maternity leave. Argentinean women get not only the same three months of paid leave, but also reimbursement for their child-care costs for the first five years of their children's lives. And in Chile, where per-capita income is about one quarter what it is in the United States, the law protects a woman's job for up to one year after she has a baby.

The Czech Republic, which has a below-average per-capita income for Europe, has nevertheless arranged for working parents there to have a level of flexibility Americans still can't dream of. Parents can choose their form of paid leave, having it stretch from one to three years. (The shorter leave comes with a higher pay, while the longer one is paid at a lower rate.) In recognition of the fact that few people can accurately predict the particular needs of the child or the desires of the parent beforehand, the program allows families to choose the form of leave they want up to six months after a child is born.

Several other countries give financial support that isn't connected to employment. Australia, for instance, pays parents a "baby bonus" regardless of their work status. And Finland has a form of at-home infant care not unlike New Mexico's AHIC program, although the program's benefits extend to all citizens. After a Finnish mother has had her 17.5 weeks of paid maternity leave and 26 weeks of paid parental leave and her husband has taken his 4 weeks of paid paternity leave, the mother can return to work and receive government-subsidized child care. But a mother or a father also has the option of instead receiving a stipend while staying home until a child is three years old. (If the parent chooses to work part-time, the benefit could extend until the child turns seven.) The government essentially pays a parent the money that would have gone to pay for the child's spot in a national child-care system if he or she returned to work.

. . .

Here, in the United States, Bernadette Cano has never held a job that included a single week of paid leave, let alone three years of subsidized time at home with kids. If she had the chance, she says she would spend every single day with her young children until they're old enough to go to school. "And then I'd be waiting in the parking lot," says Cano, a twenty-two-year-old with a serious expression, who wears her black hair in a tight ponytail. But fantasize though she may about the life of a stay-at-home mom, Cano is working full-time at a Wal-Mart not far from Lopez's trailer in New Mexico. Last year, when she had a two-year-old and was pregnant with her second, Cano worked in her job in the fitting room until eight hours before going into labor. She used vacation and personal days that she had saved during the course of a year to take five weeks off after her second son was born.

Technically, Cano was entitled to the full twelve weeks guaranteed by the FMLA (Wal-Mart, of course, employs more than fifty people, and Cano had worked there full-time for more than a year), but she feared that she would have to foreclose on the trailer and the surrounding land she had recently purchased with her boyfriend if she went any longer than she did without a paycheck. Cano says she tried to steel herself for the early separation from her baby, but the physical and emotional reality of being apart from her little son was worse than she had feared. "I thought I'd be able to handle it," she said during a lunch break at the McDonald's inside Wal-Mart, her eyes welling up with tears even though months had passed since her first day back. But when she returned to the superstore, where her responsibilities include taking clothes from customers and tidying up the fitting room, she was both physically exhausted and achingly sad about having to leave her newborn so soon.

"I was thinking about the baby all the time," Cano says quietly.

She was also still feeling the effects of a difficult labor, in which she bled extensively and had to have two transfusions. Cano had headaches and was weak for her first two to three weeks back at work. Although she says she generally enjoys her big-box retail job, it felt torturous when she first returned. Luckily, Cano's boyfriend, Peter, was able to look after their son when she was at work, even though such stints cut into his own sleep time (he leaves for his overnight job as a security guard when she arrives at home). But even though she knew her newborn was in good hands, she was so preoccupied with his well-being that she jeopardized her job to check on him. "We're not supposed to have cell phones," she says. "But sometimes in the beginning I would bring mine and sneak a text message to make sure everything's okay and find out what they're up to."

While a luckier woman might spend her first postnatal months bonding with her newborn and being nursed back to health herself, Cano was soon back to work "as if nothing had happened," as she puts it. Ideally, she would have eased back into work gradually, with part-time hours and a private space where she could pump breast milk. Instead, when she went back, Cano immediately resumed her unforgiving and unpredictable schedule. Some days she works from 2 to 11 p.m., others from 7 a.m. to 4 p.m., 12 p.m. to 9 p.m., or 10 a.m. to 7 p.m. And on the many nights that her supervisors judge the departments to be inadequately cleaned or the shelves not fully stocked, she has to stay even past the scheduled end of the shift to work overtime with little forewarning. Sometimes she gets home so late, Peter has to arrange for his mother to drive half an hour and stay with the children until Cano gets home.

Wal-Mart spokesperson John Simley says that the company's policy is to provide employees with twelve weeks of unpaid job-protected leave of absence for pregnancy and childbirth, which amounts to following the law. He also notes that the company has instituted a new scheduling system, which posts shifts three weeks in advance and is designed to help workers get work hours that are most convenient for them. But Cano says that although she has advance knowledge of her schedule, she finds it extremely difficult to get any changes or shift swaps approved. "So," she says, "I work whatever they give me."

Perla Saenz had a similarly traumatic experience after the birth of her second child. A twenty-seven-year-old mother of two, Saenz returned to work at a small pharmacy in Arizona, just four weeks after her son was delivered by cesarean section—and two weeks after her incision from that surgery reopened. (She heard her older son gag in the night and, without pausing to remember her doctor's warning against lifting anything heavier than ten pounds, instinctively picked him up.) But despite the gaping wound on her belly, which her doctor thought best not to sew up again for fear of infection, and her strong desire to stay home with her children, Saenz was all too soon back on her feet. She had been without work before. And with the two little ones, she needed the income and the job that much more. Perhaps it was the physical trauma that brought on the illness she had in those first weeks back at work. Or maybe it was the emotional strain of being apart from her newborn before she was ready. Whatever the cause, those first two months back at work were nightmarish; she stood behind the counter in the pharmacy, often feverish, dizzy, exhausted, and sore from her slowly healing wound.

Although professional women who can afford to take their full FMLA leave have the "gold standard" within our time-starved work culture, many of them feel that three months isn't enough time away from work. Whether or not they're satisfied with the duration of their leaves, returning to work after having a baby can be extremely traumatic, especially if a woman goes from being home full-time with her child one day to working full-time the next. The emotional path through that abrupt transition can be full of surprising mood swings, which is perhaps why so many of the women I spoke with about it sounded as if they were two people in the course of one interview. Often they started out sounding upbeat, describing themselves as lucky and content, only to follow these positive statements with despairing ones.

Take Liz Mahaffey, a television executive in New York, who began by saying that she was pretty happy working full-time with a young child and then went on to describe certain moments within her return to her job when her daughter was three and a half months old as "a depth of misery I've never experienced before." She has a trusted babysitter who cares for her daughter during the day, an arrangement she summed up as "really good," before adding that "There are times at work when you realize you're just sitting there when you could be with your child. You don't know the look on her face and you can't really know. You'll never really know. I've never felt so conflicted about how I'm leading my life."

No doubt, part of the ambivalence stems from the fact that while their situations may be difficult, so many other working women are in worse straits. Their relative privilege makes women feel so bad for less-fortunate working moms that, as Mahaffey puts it, "It's hard to complain."

Indeed, Mahaffey is acutely aware of how much better her situation is compared to those of other mothers in her office. Because she is a valued employee, she negotiated a deal in which she's allowed to work at home two days a week—at least, theoretically. In reality, she usually works at home only one day a week, during which she is really working and not caring for her daughter. Still, she has considerably more time at home than many of the other working mothers she knows. And she tends to leave work at 5 p.m., while many other moms in her office stay as late as 8 p.m.

"It breaks my heart when I walk out of the office and see them still working," she says. "We went through our pregnancies together and had babies together, and I'm going home to mine and they're still sitting there."

During the first months after having a child, many women feel they have no alternative but to work full-time, which is another root of their conflicted emotions. Because their incomes pay the bills and perhaps also because they don't want to sacrifice the satisfaction gained from a hard-earned career, they simply don't see another way of doing things. Yet despite their resignation, many of the professional mothers of infants I spoke with said they would, if it were possible, organize their lives differently—well, eventually, they often said that. At first, when asked to envision their ideal situations, most women had a hard time imagining what they wanted beyond what's realistically possible.

Such was the case for Heather Schwartz, a mother of two who works between forty-five and sixty-five hours per week as a designer for a pharmaceutical advertising firm. Initially, she said her dream would be a life in which she could set her own hours every day. Nothing more? I asked. After pausing for several minutes to puzzle over the concept, Schwartz decided that she would take a day off a week. A moment later, she changed that to a half-time schedule that would allow her "equal amounts of time to work and do play dates."

Back in reality, Schwartz, who has an eight-month-old and a three-year-old, says there are plenty of nights when she stays in the office until two or three in the morning. Nevertheless, she is relatively content with her current work arrangement, primarily because her schedule was so much worse at her previous job, also in advertising. When she returned to that position as the mother of a thirteen-week-old, she was desperately hoping to keep her hours to a realistic minimum, which meant coming in to the office at 9:30 a.m. and leaving around 6:30 p.m., in addition to working a full day on every other weekend. But her dream of working between forty-five and fifty-three hours a week was dashed by her boss. Instead, many days she worked well into the night, and saw her daughter only during the forty-five minutes she was scurrying around the house getting ready to leave for work. She often cried on the way to and from the office and quit five weeks after going back.

Part of what can make a woman's plunge back into work so excruciating when she has a young baby is that it is, most often, a plunge. Rather than starting part-time and working up to a full-time schedule, most workers resume the daily grind as if, as Bernadette Cano put it, nothing happened. Coreen Kremer, a technical publications supervisor for a semiconductor company in Irvine, California, remembers her first days back as dizzyingly busy. "Bam! You have projects dumped in your lap. You have fires to put out," she says.

And although she often worried and wondered about her four-month-old son, she knew better than to show it. "You have to put your game face on."

At her television job, Liz Mahaffey got the message right away. "They'll look at pictures the first day, and then after that, they don't want to hear about it," she says. "My boss hasn't asked about the baby since I got back." Nor has Mahaffey mentioned the little one. And when Schwartz went looking for another job in advertising after quitting, she knew better than to bring up that she had an eight-month-old during the interview process—and, since being hired, has mostly kept the existence of her young children under wraps.

Still, it can be hard for the mothers of young babies to slip completely back into work mode, particularly if they have to wake up during the night to feed their newborns, as many of them do. When Elizabeth Madden returned to work full-time doing organizational development for a large public accounting firm in Southern California three months after giving birth, she came up with a slogan for her new life: "Four hours of sleep and four cups of coffee." In addition to her infant son, who still wakes up to nurse three times a night, Madden has a two-year-old daughter and a spouse who travels for work about half the time. Madden says sleep deprivation has taken such a toll on her short-term memory that she now makes a list of all the tasks she needs to do and people she needs to speak with and carries it with her at all times in the office.

Although Madden is grateful for the overall understanding she's received from her colleagues and employers, she says she was disappointed by the lack of support she got for pumping breast milk at work. "It would have been nice if someone would have said 'Welcome back to work. Do you need a room to nurse in?'" she says. Instead, because her office doesn't have a lock, she ended up jamming a chair against the door while she pumped. She is not alone in encountering hurdles in trying to keep up nursing while working full-time.

Pumping milk for a caregiver to feed the baby later is supposedly a simple way for working women to follow the advice of infant health experts.

The practical reality of pumping at work, however, is often far more complicated.

Many offices don't have a private place to do it, so women are relegated to restrooms, cubicles, or even, in some cases, supply closets. Electric breast pumps are heavy, as women who lug them to and from work know. And even the best pumps are less effective than babies at keeping breast milk flowing. Eventually, supply usually dwindles, which makes babies less interested in nursing, which in turn makes it harder to produce milk and hastens the end of breast-feeding altogether.

Despite the fact that the American Academy of Pediatrics recommends that babies get breast milk for at least a year, the absence of any national protections for a woman's right to breast-feed in the workplace and the lack of accommodations by individual employers makes it extremely difficult to maintain the ability to nurse for so long. Among the dozens of working mothers I spoke with, most threw in the towel (or the breast pump) well before six months, complaining of obstacles like glass-walled offices, frenetic work schedules, and inconsiderate colleagues. As Terra Lynch, a teacher in a New York City public high school, explained, a stressful workplace isn't conducive to lactating. Lynch had to pump in the office of a female colleague. Although the office offered a much-needed door, the colleague would sometimes talk about work while Lynch was pumping. "If she did, there'd be a two-ounce difference," Lynch recalls. "When I could just relax and think about my daughter, I'd get more milk."

Jenny Shepherd, an account manager for Dow Jones who works in Southern California, says she stopped pumping after a coworker barged in on her doing it in a conference room. Another mom summed up the obstacles to pumping, by explaining that because she had to go into another room and couldn't answer e-mails while she did it, work simply "won out" over breast-feeding within a few weeks of her return to her job.

For infants, the physical benefits of nursing are potentially considerable: breast-fed babies are less likely to get both respiratory and digestive illnesses. But women can get a lot out of breast-feeding, too, and sometimes suffer when they can't nurse. Many say the guilt and sadness over having to stop breast-feeding was the hardest part of returning to work. Indeed, the emotions that wash over a woman on ending a time spent mostly with her baby and beginning one spent mostly away from that baby are intense, especially since most new mothers are still adjusting to the role of motherhood. "How on earth are you supposed to process all this info, this total change of life, and come back and be productive at your job?" asks Mahaffey, the TV executive. "You're still integrating all these parts of yourself."

While American women often have to work during the first forty days after birth, most other cultures treat this immediate postnatal period as a sacred time, in which both the new mother and the baby receive help and special attention.

Throughout history and all over the world, people have tended to carve out at least a minimum of six weeks in which women are exempt from responsibilities other than child care, according to Malin Eberhard-Gran, a Norwegian public health scholar who has compiled a cross-cultural comparison of postnatal practices. Indeed, in the Bible, it was forty days before Mary was purified after the virgin birth, and this is also the length of the rest period observed in Islam. In many Latin American cultures, the same period is observed and referred to as *la cuarantena*, which comes from the Spanish word for "forty." In some other cultures, women are granted special treatment for even longer. In Japan and India, for instance, women typically go to their mothers' homes for several months after giving birth, while in Nigeria women dwell in special "fattening rooms," where they are spared responsibilities other than eating, sleeping, and caring for their babies.[10]

Research has shown that this time to recover after birth and focus on a new baby can spare women some serious mental health problems. One study of Mexican women in the United States showed that those who followed the rules of *la cuarantena* reported less depression in the postpartum period. Whether paid or unpaid, longer maternity leaves are associated with a decline in depressive symptoms, a reduction in the likelihood of severe depression, and an improvement in overall maternal health, according to a 2008 working paper issued by the National Bureau of Economic Research.[11] Shorter maternity leaves also affect the relationships between mothers and their infants. Mothers who returned to work before their babies were six months old were less likely to play with, tickle, hug, and engage in cognitively stimulating activities with their babies, according to a 2006 study by Child Trends, a nonprofit research center that focuses on child development.[12]

Not surprisingly, the nature and intensity of the work situation that women return to also matter. Mothers of nine-month-olds who worked more than forty hours a week were more likely to be depressed than were those who worked forty hours or less, according to same Child Trends study. It sounds obvious: that mothers suffer if they spend too much time away from their newborns. Yet a bizarre, punishing disregard for the impact of work stress on mothers of very young children permeates our culture. How else can one explain the U.S. Army's policy of sending female soldiers back into a war zone only four months after giving birth? Female soldiers have six weeks off before they have to return to training full-time. At least in theory, they could still continue pumping breast milk during this training period and see their babies and nurse when not on duty. Once deployed a little more than nine weeks later, though, women have no time with their newborns, whether for nursing or for bonding of any kind.

Welfare policy reflects a similar disconnect from the reality of motherhood. When work requirements for welfare recipients first began, as far back as 1967, women who had young children were granted permission to stay home to parent. But as more middle-class women have entered the workforce and encountered rigidity around their own ability to take time off after having children, the length of the exemption from work requirements that is allowed to welfare recipients has shrunk. Under the Work Incentives Program, which imposed education and training requirements on welfare recipients, the federal government allowed women with children under six to be exempt from such responsibilities. Then, in 1988, the Family Support Act lowered the age limit, so, in order to continue receiving aid, mothers had to return to their assigned positions when their children turned three. With the passage of the Welfare Reform Act in 1996, the feds did away with exemptions for mothers altogether, leaving the issue up to the states.

Now some states, including New Mexico, allow women a twelve-month exception from work requirements after having a child (this comes with a lifetime limit, so that if a woman takes six months off after each of two children, on having the third she is not entitled to any additional time off), but many other states are not even this generous. In twelve states, women have to return to their work assignments in three months or less. And in six states, they are guaranteed no leave at all from their work assignments after having babies. That can mean having to leave newborns only days after giving birth.

Such was the case in Montana, where women received no official exemption from work requirements until 2008, when a new law granted mothers three to four months off after having children. As a result, many women had to return to work almost immediately after giving birth, a brutal situation made even more difficult by a shortage of infant care. "We have moms who have had their babies and five days later they're in the worksite," explains Mary Caferro, a lobbyist for Working for Equality and Economic Liberation, or WEEL, an organization started by welfare moms in Montana. "Many low-income folks here work in jobs with nontraditional hours. And we have very little care provided after six, so people piece together solutions to child care—one night here, two nights there. Or infants are in the care of older siblings."

In response, WEEL spearheaded its own at-home infant-care program in 2002, which served as a model for New Mexico's program. The idea was to create a pool of money that would allow welfare recipients to use parenting to fulfill their work requirement so they could stay home until their children were two years old. The stipend wasn't much—just $375 per month for each child, the market rate for what someone would be paid for looking after a baby that wasn't her own. But the money, which was ultimately made available to anyone making up to 150 percent of the poverty level (which, for a family of four, was $27,366 at the time), clearly helped women survive a life transition that's stressful under even the best circumstances.

In New Mexico, there's no question that AHIC has made Lopez's life more pleasant and bearable than it was when her boys were Carissa's age. Lopez thinks the time she's spent playing with her daughter might even have helped Carissa hit developmental milestones more quickly than her sons did, although she allows for the possibility that it just seems that way because "I'm here to see it this time." Carissa has also had fewer colds and "hasn't gotten her asthma yet," as Lopez puts it, referring to the ailment as an eventuality she's come to assume her children will endure.

And, of course, Carissa has yet to go to day care, which, for Lopez, is a relief. In the past, she's found herself in a situation that might be called "musical babies." As many low-income moms do, she had to put her own children in child care so she could work taking care of other people's children as a child-care worker. Her preference to be with her own children was intensified when her sons returned from their center with bruises. By the time Carissa was born, Kalen had worked in child care for several years and was well aware of the range of people her daughter might encounter, from the most loving and experienced caretakers to hardhearted, depressed, and even violent ones.

The Lopezes' life is far from perfect. Kalen spends a lot of time in the car, driving to pick up her husband from graduate school, where he's training to be a fifth-grade teacher, or shuttling the boys to football and baseball practices. But Carissa is almost always right there with Lopez, even when the child is only fussing in her car seat. Their near-constant togetherness has made it possible for Kalen to continue breast-feeding Carissa longer than she did either of the boys. Most of all, their time spent cuddling, playing, and hanging out has allowed them to be "really, really close," something she missed out on with her baby boys.

When Susan Loubet peddles the value of AHIC to lawmakers, she infuses her economic arguments with the idea that babies and parents have a unique potential for attachment. Loubet, the driving force behind New Mexico's at-home infant care program and a lobbyist for the nonprofit advocacy group the New Mexico Women's Agenda, has tried to translate the value of this relationship into dollars saved down the road, arguing that increased bonding will ultimately lower the costs of dealing with dysfunctional citizens later in life. "It all comes back to bonding," she says, after ticking off the possibilities for savings—in prison and mental health costs, for instance—when these securely attached babies grow up to be healthy adults who don't land in institutions.

A gray-haired feminist, Loubet was able to stay home when her son Thom, now thirty-four, was an infant. In what now sounds like a rose-colored vision of 1970s parenting, she took a job at *Ms.* magazine when Thom turned one and brought her son with her to the office while she worked as an assistant to Gloria Steinem. Employees at all levels of the magazine helped out with Thom and Alex, the young son of another employee. The child-friendly office workers even filled an extension of the publicity department with toys, turning it into an indoor "tot lot," where Thom and Alex happily played when they weren't riding little scooters and bikes in and out of various offices.

Loubet now sees the time she spent with Thom, both at home and in the office, as part of her motivation for starting AHIC in New Mexico. "My husband and I said to each other that this was our kid and we didn't want to blow it," Loubet recalls of her decision to have Thom spend as much time as possible with his immediate family in his early years. "I guess I want everyone to be able to say that: this is my kid and I don't want to blow it."

But in reality many parents are still left feeling as if they've "blown it." The handful of states that have attempted AHIC programs have made them available to only the poorest of the poor, and a proposal for a national AHIC-style program would do the same. Even when combined with the Family Medical and Medical Leave Act, these programs leave the vast economic middle of new American mothers without decent options after they give birth.

Translating Loubet's lofty feminist ideals into actual policy turns out to be fairly complicated in other ways, too. For one thing, despite its cuddly connotations, bonding may be the touchiest issue in child development. There's little question that even early on, babies have an intense attachment to their primary caretakers. As child development expert T. Berry Brazelton has documented in a video he made to push for paid leave legislation in 1987, at just two months of age, a child can already be deeply attached to his mother. When she leaves the room, the baby looks sad. His face "puckers up," as Brazelton recently described it to me, and when she returns, "He looks at her as if to say 'where have you been all this time?'" Brazelton believes that both mothers and fathers should spend significant time with babies. And John Bowlby, known as the father of attachment theory, was careful to specify that "mothering" care needn't always be provided by the child's actual mother. Yet many people have a more essentialist take on the concept, arguing that women and only women should be raising their children and turning the seemingly innocuous term *bonding* into a hand grenade tossed back and forth in the battle over working motherhood.

Hitched to the delicate issue of bonding, at-home-infant-care programs can get mucked up in such double-edged arguments about stay-at-home motherhood that all too often leave working women feeling terrible. Despite being open to both fathers and mothers of young children, the majority of participants in at-home-infant-care programs thus far have been women. It's undoubtedly the sense that these programs help cement women's rightful place on the domestic front that appeals to its conservative proponents, such as the right-wing lawmakers in Montana, for instance, who liked the idea of helping women stay at home to raise children and joined forces with self-proclaimed feminist welfare recipients to get AHIC off the ground there.

At-home infant care also has its opponents. Some worry that it contains an implicit criticism of working mothers. (If children are best cared for by their own mothers—or even by their fathers—then what of all the parents who cannot or choose not to stay home with their babies?) Others have more practical concerns, particularly that enrollment in some programs has been low because of the piddling amount of the stipend.

It's true that AHIC programs don't have anywhere near the funding they'd need to make them viable. New Mexico offers such a small monthly stipend that many women choose not to participate when they realize they wouldn't be able to supplement it with work. Families receive only $250 a week, an amount that for some reason program staff members insist should not be used to pay bills. (It's hard to imagine living below the poverty line and not considering every penny as potential help in covering costs.) Montana and Minnesota, which also had AHIC programs, gave only slightly higher stipends and are no longer in existence because they didn't get funding to continue. Even the national AHIC-style proposal, which Hillary Clinton put forward during her presidential bid, didn't include anywhere near the dollar amount necessary to make it a real option for many people.

Meanwhile, the political will to pay for such programs is unlikely to coalesce if, as AHIC does, they cover only a small segment of the population. Because mothers in well-paid jobs are in many ways in the same boat as those in lower-paying ones and even those on welfare, any policy that allows only a small minority of women time at home breeds resentment. And that, in turn, limits the possibilities for addressing the lack of maternity leave shared by women up and down the economic spectrum. Consider the experience of Don Friedman, an advocate for welfare recipients who was lobbying the New York State government after the federal welfare reform law was passed in 1996. Early the next year, Friedman, who was then working for the Community Food Resource Center, was in the state capital trying to convince legislators to grant mothers who receive what was then called Temporary Assistance for Needy Families at least one year off after giving birth. His efforts failed; the state ultimately passed a law granting an absence of no more than three months from work requirements, and Friedman attributes most of the resistance to the proposal to female staffers who worked on the issue.

"Some of the key people we dealt with were women who were particularly sensitive to" the issue of maternity leave, recalls Friedman. "They were saying, 'We're hard workers and we only get three months off. You're asking us for these people who are not working to have a year off. I'm not going to stick my neck out to get something that I can't get.'"

In New Mexico, the architects of AHIC are aware of the distaste for the idea of paying women to take care of their own children. The fear is that it harks back to the welfare system of yore, which was seen by many as engendering helplessness and laziness by rewarding poor women who stayed out of the workforce. As one dubious New Mexico lawmaker put it during a debate over the program, "We're taxing middle-income people to pay women to stay home and have babies." Even Loretta Lucero, who has an important role in overseeing AHIC as a supervisor from the state Child Care Services Bureau, has voiced concerns that the program returns women to "welfare of the '60s."

Along with budget constraints, this taint may be responsible for keeping New Mexico's stay-at-home experiment as small as it is. But an even bigger obstacle to the program may be that policy makers have so few reference points for anything between the old welfare and the newer "plunge" models. While so many other countries have managed to find middle-ground alternatives that allow both new mothers and new fathers relatively long stretches with their babies before ultimately returning to their jobs, the United States has little between the polar extremes of being forced almost immediately either back into work or out of it altogether. If we could fill in the holes between them with more reasonable options, people such as Kalen Lopez and Devorah Gartner, who want and need to spend significant amounts of time with their young children—and want and need to continue working—wouldn't be seen as lazy, spoiled, or even lucky. They'd simply be seen as parents.

7

Good Day Care Is Hard to Find

The Working Mom Crisis

Alexandria, a pudgy ten-month-old with pink bows clipped to her tiny ponytails, is waiting. Propped up on a pillow in the tidy living room of her apartment in Palm Beach, Florida, she's calmly swigging warm formula, while her mother gets ready for work. Soon she'll be buckled into her car seat and whisked off. To where? She must wait to find out. Most days she goes to a lady's house a few minutes away, but sometimes she winds up at her uncle's apartment or with a friend of her mom's, if one will take her. If she could, Alexandria might tell you that what she's really waiting for is one safe place to be every day while her mother works. And she might have to wait a very long time.

Alexandria is on the waiting list for subsidized care, along with more than forty-five thousand other children in Florida and almost half a million around the country. Countless families could use serious help with child-care costs. Working parents now spend more on child care than they do on college tuition, food, car payments, and, in forty-nine states, rent. Yet even though some child-care subsidies are available, which might allow us to feel as if we've begun to solve the problem, the amount of money falls far short of reaching all who meet the strict income criteria set by states to sift out the neediest of needy families. The rest remain on wait lists, like Alexandria's mother, Denise, who is raising four children while working full-time as an assistant case worker for a family service agency. Having earned only $19,000 last year, Denise is eligible for aid, and she made sure to request it right after her daughter was born. But still she and Alexandria wait.

Across the country, families in dire financial situations qualify for help but don't get it because of a lack of funding for child care. Of the more than fifteen million children who were entitled to child-care help nationwide in 2000, only one out of seven received it, according to the Washington-based advocacy group the Center for Law and Social Policy.[1] And since then, the share of needy families getting help seems to have gotten even smaller.[2] In a slight nod of recognition to the difficulty of affording decent care on low wages, the federal government has been offering child-care subsidies to some of the poorest working families since at least 1974. Yet while both the number of women in the workforce and the price of care relative to wages have shot up since then, government spending on day care hasn't risen accordingly. The backup steadily worsened during the Bush administrations, when there were no significant increases in funding for child care.

Nowhere is the need for a unified, national approach to helping families clearer than in child care. You'd expect good child care to be expensive. But for many families, the high cost of good care simply places it out of reach. And even with the priciest (a Manhattan center I visited that charged $23,000 per child annually comes to mind), it's hard to be sure what you're getting. There are no federal regulations or even federal standards for child care.

Because government has understandably focused most of the little it spends on child care helping the poorest families, most other parents find themselves in a terrible bind, having too high an income to qualify for subsidized care, yet making too little money to afford the entire cost themselves. Our national "solution" thus far has been to treat child care as a commodity. Yet the market approach has left most families unable to afford care—or decent care, anyway. So widespread and desperate is the need for cash, Citibank has come up with a special loan to help pay for it. The Web site for the I Pay Childcare loan urges parents to "afford the best childcare possible," cleverly touching on the well-known importance of what goes on in the early years and the incredible range of quality in child care that exists. Pay more, is the implication—and, often, the reality—and your kid might get a decent leg up.

Meanwhile, the little public assistance that is available comes through a confused and starved "system" of more than a dozen different funding streams that go to programs run in countless different settings, including community organizations, day-care centers, and public schools. Advocates have spent years bogged down in this depressing culture of scarcity, fighting over crumbs of public funding for their various tiny constituents. Those making the case for the "zero-to-three" crowd fiercely argue on behalf of infants and toddlers, while others see spending on the littlest ones as taking away from the pot that is available for four- and five-year-old preschoolers.

The lack of decent, affordable child care in the United States makes it hard for any working mother to feel good about her situation, whether she's employed because of a desire for personal fulfillment, out of economic need, or some mix of the two. Without reasonable child-care options, women often feel like the fault is theirs, that they have erred by choosing bad providers, by managing their time poorly, or by simply working at all. This is yet another case of a public policy problem masquerading as a personal failing. And, again, it hurts not just mothers, but their children, too.

Consider what happens to the babies, toddlers, and preschool-age kids who don't get subsidized care while their parents are at work. Some, like Cassie Hinckson's one-year-old quadruplets, spend much of their time effectively on their own. For the first year of their lives, Hinckson, a single mom who works the night shift at a home for mentally ill substance abusers, had help from a home health aide. But the union to which she belonged paid the aide for only a year and, after that, she and her four small children were pretty much on their own. Her mother was able to stay with the babies from midnight until eight-thirty in the morning, when Hinckson returned home from work and her mother went to her own job. But because Hinckson earned too much to qualify for child-care help and too little to pay for it on her own, she had no help during the days after being up all night working. So, on most days during the year before their second birthday, the children more or less entertained themselves, somehow miraculously avoiding serious harm.

"I'd go into the room and hope for the best," remembers Hinckson. "I'd turn on the cartoons and lock the bedroom door and hope and pray that nothing happened." What did these tiny children, born little more than a year earlier, actually do when left to their own devices? Knock each other over? Eat little bits of lint from the floor? Tussle over toys? No one knows for sure, not even their mother. Occasionally, she was jolted awake by a cry and staggered sleepily over to the baby who was insistent on getting his or her momentary need met. But mostly, she slept.

Other children wind up going to work with their parents, as Alexandria did on this particular Friday morning in Palm Beach. Her usual setup is far from ideal. The woman who cares for her is elderly, leaves the TV on for much of the day, and charges $150 a week, which strains Denise's tight budget. Perhaps most frustrating, the woman is sometimes unavailable, as she is today. Thankfully, Denise has a plan B: Alexandria's uncle agreed to look after the baby just this morning. But when she calls him repeatedly from her car as she heads toward his apartment, he doesn't answer his phone.

What's a woman who's late for work to do when her babysitters go AWOL? Denise pulls into a gas station to ponder this question. If she brings Alexandria along on her workday, which begins with three hours of driving to pick up a child in foster care and bring him to visit his mother, she may risk losing her job. But she doesn't know any other trustworthy babysitters. And the choice between endangering her job or her baby is an easy one. So, as she's done on more than one occasion in the past, she heaves a big sigh and drives off to work with her infant daughter in the backseat.

Other children on the waiting list, like little one-and-a-half-year-old Valerie, a smiley toddler whose dark hair is cut in a pageboy, go to decent preschools at great expense to their parents.

Four out of every ten single mothers who pay for child care spend half or more of their incomes on it.

Still, some can afford only the dicier options. Valerie's mom, Glabedys, who lives alone with Valerie and doesn't get child support, is pleased with the center where her daughter spends her days. When she drops Valerie off at Busy Bees Preschool, housed in two toy-filled buildings in Wilton Manors, Valerie runs off to play, instead of crying and clinging to her mother, as she used to do when she was left with neighbors. She's been learning about colors and shapes, and she clearly likes her teachers.

But while Valerie remains on the waiting list for a subsidy to pay for her care, Glabedys pays her preschool fees with money she would have spent on groceries. Although she works full-time at a factory that makes hurricane-protection gates, she couldn't even afford her apartment after the $135-a-week outlay to Busy Bees. So she rented a storage place for most of her things and a small room in a house where the two now live. They survive on donations from a local food pantry.

Some other parents who can't afford care go into debt, putting the fees for child care on their credit cards. (The "I Pay Childcare" program, by the way, offers a dedicated credit card for child care.) Still others leave children home with older siblings—a phenomenon that contributes to the state's truancy problem, according to local child advocates. And some mothers stay home with their children despite a desperate need for income. Not surprisingly, research has shown that parents who receive help paying for child care are more likely to be employed and to have higher incomes.[3]

For many who don't get help, the options are few and often lead to terrible tradeoffs. Such is the case for Heather Thomlinson, the mother of sixteen-month-old Ian and a school-age daughter in Fort Lauderdale. Her family of four is living on the extremely variable paycheck of her boyfriend, who installs leather upholstery in cars and is paid by the car. Even on good weeks, his income barely covers the family's expenses. So Thomlinson applied for help with child care when Ian was born. Yet she's still on the waiting list, caught in a sort of catch-22: She can't envision how to afford care that would enable her to interview for a job, let alone keep it. But because she doesn't work, she has been labeled a low priority on the waiting list. So, the family ekes by. The other week, Thomlinson had only eight diapers to last her son for three days. "I had to leave each one on a little longer than I should have," she says. "Eventually, he got a rash."

Unfortunately, Ian's diaper rash, the quadruplets' unsupervised days, and Valerie's donated food get no airtime in the national shouting match over child care, or at least not in the mainstream media coverage, which seems to be an endless loop of condemnations and defenses of both day care and working mothers. In the most recent installment, researcher Jay Belsky, a founder and long-time investigator in a federal study of child care, warned parents that children who spent time in the care of anyone except their mothers were more likely than those cared for by stay-at-home moms to exhibit bad behavior, both as preschoolers and as kindergartners. Despite the fact that he disagreed with his coauthors of the federal study on both the existence of the finding and its implications, the link between day care and bad behavior made it into headlines across the country. And a chorus of conservatives quickly chimed in to declare day care a bad thing.

Meanwhile, there was little mention of the fact that there are great variations in child care or that children in good care tend to do better. In fact, being in consistent and emotionally supportive care has been shown to help improve preschoolers' cognitive functioning, peer relationships, and language skills.

In fact, the clear association between better care and better outcomes is one of the main—and, in contrast to the Belsky scare, widely accepted—truths to emerge from the same research, the Study of Early Child Care and Youth Development. This finding has two important corollaries, both of which the country seems to have a hard time stomaching. First, that good care in which children do well costs money. There's plenty of research on what that good care should entail. Among other things, young children need one-on-one attention; consistent relationships with trained, knowledgeable adults; and safe environments, complete with educational toys and books, all of which are expensive.

The second reality that is perhaps even more difficult to confront, especially for proponents of child care, is that without these expenditures, child care can be pretty bad. And it's not only kids on the waiting list whose parents can't afford much who are in lousy care. Parents who are lucky enough to get subsidies can use them to pay any center- or home-based day care. Although regulated providers must technically meet minimum requirements set by the state, the lack of funding for wages, training, and monitoring severely limits their ability to meet even those. As a result, the federal government now pays for many child-care situations that span the gamut from worrisome to horrendous.

Even by the federal government's own accounting, our nation's child care leaves much to be desired. According to research done by the National Institute of Child Health and Human Development in 2000, the quality of most care across the country is either fair (53 percent) or poor (8 percent). But Florida may offer some of the starkest examples because of the rates that providers are paid for subsidized kids, which vary from county to county but are shockingly low throughout the state. In Miami/Dade County, for instance, the state pays providers just $1.85 an hour for each subsidized toddler, or $2.12 for an infant, which means that centers tend to pay their employees only the state's minimum wage, $7.72 per hour. Not surprisingly, there is a severe, chronic shortage of qualified people who have the patience, skills, and willingness to work with young children for so little money. Denise, Alexandria's mom, is already well aware of the problem. Two years ago, she moved her three older children out of a center where they were getting subsidized care after they complained repeatedly of being hit by a teacher.

The eight babies in cribs at the Discovery Me Preschool in the Kendall section of Miami were too young to complain, although they made it clear with their tears and outstretched arms that they'd much rather be held or played with than confined to their tiny beds. Discovery Me, housed in a large, windowless space in a mall in Kendall, a suburban community in the southwest part of the city, provides care to fifty-two children. Officially, there should have been no more than four infants for every adult. But here there were eight alone with a single caretaker on a recent afternoon, each whiling away the hours wearing only a diaper.

Indeed, a few unannounced visits to some of the centers that accept subsidized children in Southern Florida revealed that it's not unusual for such absurd numbers of children to be in the care of a lone adult. In the Sunshine State, one child-care provider can legally look after as many as eleven two-year-olds, fifteen three-year-olds, or twenty four-year-olds. You might think it'd be impossible to surpass these state-set limits, which are the laxest in the nation. It's hard to imagine any adult keeping up with the diaper changing for eleven two-year-olds, let alone providing "quality child care to enhance the development, including language, cognitive, motor, social, and self-help skills of children," which is how Florida law describes the purpose of its child-care subsidies. Yet even these ridiculous—if not outright dangerous—ratios are routinely violated.

At the Peter Pan Child Development Center in Pompano Beach, Florida, for example, nineteen three- and four-year-olds and a school-age girl were in a small room with an elderly woman in a wheelchair on a recent afternoon. Although it was supposed to be naptime, several children strayed from their sleeping mats. Across a small walkway, another classroom full of children at the center was also understaffed, with two adults overseeing four infants and thirteen one- and two-year-olds.

Meanwhile, at Discovery Me, the ratios were even more disturbing. When I visited, Olga Ceballos, the center's director, told me that thirty-eight two-, three-, and four-year-olds had been in the care of only two adults earlier that day. Ceballos said that one of her teachers had a doctor's appointment, leaving the preschool more understaffed than usual.

There is no pool of substitute teachers for Ceballos to draw on; with the measly wages, it's hard enough to find regular staff. So the director stepped in to look after the children at one point. "There were just so many kids, I had to put the TV on," she says. Afterward, the children went into the playground adjoining the school's parking lot. Being responsible for more than two dozen running, jumping, and potentially hitting, falling, or biting toddlers was so stressful—and the risk of injury so present—that Ceballos talks about her stint looking after the lot full of children as a physical trauma. "By the time I had to leave for my meeting, I was shaking all over," she says.

Even the best-run centers have a hard time finding qualified adults to hire. At the A-Plus Early Learning Center, in a small Tudor-style building in the middle of a housing complex in Miami, director Linda Carmona Sanchez has struggled to make the work enticing to potential staff members. Teachers there and almost everywhere in the state receive no health benefits, paid vacations, or sick leave. Despite the fact that they are subject to fingerprinting and background checks and required to take a forty-five-hour training course and undergo ongoing education, most Florida child-care workers make only about $15,500 a year for full-time work. Just across the street from A-Plus, they could easily make more serving up fries at Burger King or McDonald's. Stocking the shelves at the local Wal-Mart pays more, too. Sanchez herself, who usually put in about sixty hours a week running the center during the last ten years, has a salary of only $17,680.

Paying workers the minimum wage and cutting costs aren't enough to save many child-care centers. Around the country, as parents' work hours are scaled back, fewer are able to afford child care, and centers are reporting dramatic drops in income. As the recession forces state budgets to contract, even those that rely on government funding are in peril. In Greenville, South Carolina, for instance, state budget cuts recently forced the abrupt closure of four centers for special-needs children, leaving dozens of children without therapy and child-care services.

Some of Florida's child-care woes are its own. The state has relatively high poverty levels. And thirty-two regional networks dole out the federal dollars, as opposed to the single agency that serves the same purpose in other states, creating unnecessary administrative costs and opening the door to local corruption. In a recent Miami sting, for example, eleven people were arrested for receiving subsidies for nonexistent children.

But the crisis is also clearly a national one. A substantial minority of states, seventeen in 2008, usually have waiting lists for child-care subsidies.[4] And the cutoff for eligibility is often absurdly low, eliminating even families that clearly couldn't afford child care on their own. In several, for instance, a single mother of two with an income of $20,000 now earns too much to qualify for subsidies. Other states leave their income thresholds higher and simply cap the numbers on wait lists. Still others let their lists get impossibly long. One New York City mother I interviewed received a letter informing her that she was number 39,231 on the wait list for a child-care subsidy, which meant that her one-year-old daughter might get her due around the time she was of child-bearing age herself. The lack of federal funds has also forced child-care providers to cut workers' pay; scrimp on books, toys, and crayons; and struggle to pay their rent.

In some ways, the dilemma of finding a safe place for children becomes especially pressing once kids reach the age of three, when they start to prepare for kindergarten and life beyond it in earnest. There's no question that three- and four-year-olds are ready to benefit from real teaching, in addition to the staples of traditional babysitting: keeping kids safe, fed, rested, and entertained. Research has documented that children who attend pre-K have higher high school graduation rates, less grade repetition, better standardized test performance, and even, according to one study, lower rates of teen pregnancy than those who don't.[5]

Given the range of benefits, economists have estimated that every dollar invested in high-quality pre-K yields taxpayers up to $7 in savings by reducing the need for cash assistance, criminal justice services, and remedial education.

Based on this evidence, most states have set up prekindergarten programs in recent years or are in the process of doing it. Yet the emerging pre-K system has many of the same problems that plague care for younger children. Because we have yet to spend enough so that all children can be in pre-K, in most states, only those at the very top of the economic ladder, who can afford the market rate, and those at the bottom, who qualify for government help, wind up getting spots. Most everyone in the middle misses out.

Government-funded programs serve less than a quarter of four-year-olds (only three states currently make pre-K available to all four-year-olds) and 3 percent of three-year-olds in the United States, according to the national advocacy organization Pre-K Now. Even the so-called universal programs now in place in eight states and the District of Columbia often fall far short of providing access for all who want or need it.

On paper, New York State has universal pre-K, for instance. Yet more than ten years after having passed a law mandating prekindergarten for all four-year-olds, only 39 percent of four-year-old New Yorkers attended state-funded programs.[6] Other universal programs are truly open to all but are pathetically underfunded, leaving them unable to do a decent job. In Florida, for example, the state spent a mere $2,335 per child on pre-K in the 2006 to 2007 school year, despite the fact that educational experts say that high-quality education in that state would require an investment of at least $4,055. (The legislature cut funding for pre-K by $14 million in 2007, even as enrollment was climbing.)

Perhaps most irksome to the parents who would like to rely on them, the majority of state pre-K programs aren't full day, meaning that they don't even last the duration of the school day, which is already far shorter than most parents' workdays. Nor do they last all year, breaking during summer, although parents' jobs typically don't.

Twenty of the thirty-eight state pre-K programs now in existence have attempted to navigate the lack of adequate funding by limiting their programs to low-income children. The approach makes a certain sense. Because most legislators feel that they can't foot the bill for all kids, especially in these dire financial times, they've chosen to focus on low-income children, who are particularly prone to academic troubles and least able to afford private pre-K. But income-based pre-K programs have created a new underserved group: kids in the middle-income bracket, who also suffer the effects of relative lack of income. They perform worse than high-income children do in terms of drop-out rates, the need for special education, and being left back. Yet because of the exorbitant cost of private pre-K, which went up 60 percent between 1996 and 2006, most of these middle-income families can't afford good programs either.

Indeed, in big expensive cities, private programs that function as an alternative to public pre-K can run upward of $20,000 per year. In New York, for instance, the average cost of full-time care for a four-year-old—which includes programs that aren't geared toward development or school-readiness—was $10,541 per year, a startling 17 percent of the median income of married families with children under eighteen and more than half the median income of single parents with children under eighteen, according to 2008 census figures.[7] Yet that average includes a wide range of prices that can reach up to more than $22,000. The soaring average costs also include both low- and high-quality programs that may or may not have experienced teachers or attempt anything educational. They also typically end in the early afternoon, well before most parents' workdays are over, so full-time working parents have to pay for additional child care on top of "tuition."

Even when children hit elementary school age, they and their parents aren't out of the woods. Adept though they may be at playing video games and wielding sarcasm, older children need care and attention. While they may be better positioned to stay at home by themselves than, say, kindergarteners (1 percent of whom, incidentally, are left to care for themselves after school, according to the After-School Alliance), latchkey teens are more likely to skip school, use illegal drugs, steal, or harm someone. The few hours after school and before parents get home from work are famously the time of day when juvenile crime triples. Yet only 3 percent of the nation's high school students are in after-school programs, in which they'd be directed to do something constructive, and more than half are left to their own devices.

What happens to these older children? Some, even little ones like eight-year-old Jaelen Simms in Cincinnati, are taking care of their siblings. For five months, Jaelen was in an after-school program at a local public school. Typically, he arrived around 2:30 p.m., had a snack, got help with his homework, and then had free play time in the school gym or outside, depending on the weather, before his mother picked him up around 4 p.m. Jaelen's mom, Melanie, says he loved the program. A single mother who works as a waitress at a nearby Bob Evans restaurant, Melanie loved the program, too. While her son was in a safe place for two hours after school, she earned an additional $20 or so each day. Unfortunately, for both mother and son, the twelve-year-old girl across the street who had been walking Jaelen's four-year-old sister home after school became suddenly unable to do so, which meant that Jaelen had to give up his spot so he could walk his sister home and watch her until their mother returned from work.

Part of what's so frustrating about the nation's child-care mess is that it could be largely straightened out with adequate funding. Although the Obama administration has taken a big first step in directing $5 billion in stimulus money toward early education and child care, a total revamping to fully meet our country's child-care needs would have a much bigger price tag. According to estimates by Mark Greenberg of the Center for American Progress, it would cost $30 billion per year to both boost the quality of child care and guarantee help in paying for it to everyone with an income less than twice the poverty level, or almost one million more low-income working families.

Still, we know it's possible to provide high-quality universal or near-universal child care because many countries, such as France, Belgium, Denmark, and Sweden, have done it.

In 1971, the United States was poised to do it, too. The Comprehensive Child Care Development Act would have established child care as a right for all families, regardless of income. The broadly supported legislation was to have established national quality standards and provided money for the training of child-care providers and the purchase of facilities. Families making up to about 44 percent of the median income were to have received free care and those earning up to 74 percent would have been charged on a sliding scale. But, alas, although the bill passed both the House and the Senate, Nixon killed it, delivering a veto speech penned by Pat Buchanan that warned against "communal approaches to childrearing."

Since its 1971 defeat, engineered in part by Phyllis Schlafly, the idea of a comprehensive approach to child care has been mostly dormant—if not dead—in the United States, and another generation of women has been felled on this battleground. Substantially underfunded, what exists of federally subsidized child care is vulnerable to the conservative criticism of government services as unworthy of expansion. (Like health care, who wants second-rate services for their children, right?) And so the cycle of neglect of a government solution to the nation's child-care woes has continued since Schlafly's time.

The last decade has been an especially dark time for those who care about child care. Few ventured to even hope for a slight uptick in meager child-care assistance. Without an infusion of dollars, efforts to address the problems of quality or access rang hollow. Take the state legislation that's been wending through the Florida legislature. Supported by several lawmakers and Governor Charlie Crist, all of whom clearly recognized the need to improve the quality of child care, the bill would require all people who teach preschool-age children to hold a bachelor's degree. But the legislation would provide no pay increase for these workers.

The countries that do have more comprehensive public child-care systems all devote much more money to them than does the United States, which spends only about $200 on care for every child under fifteen, according to Janet Gornick, an expert in international social welfare policy. That's one-fifth of per-capita spending on child care in France, where 99 percent of three-, four-, and five-year-olds are enrolled in publicly provided care, and one-tenth of that in Sweden and Denmark, where virtually all preschool-age children of working parents can immediately have access to a spot.[8] Much as the education of children over five is seen here as the responsibility of taxpayers (no one expects parents alone to shoulder the actual cost of their children's elementary schooling), these countries treat the care of young children of working parents as a public responsibility and make it available to all.

Historically, twin arguments have defended such expenditures: that parents need to work and that children benefit from education before they hit school age. With some two-thirds of mothers of young children now employed, the necessity of work has never been clearer. Single mothers, such as Denise, clearly need no reminder. The parents waiting for subsidies here and across the country arguably understand the importance of work better than anyone. Were they on welfare, they'd be guaranteed low-cost child care, which, by law, comes with a workfare assignment. So, by having a low-wage job, they're already fighting a built-in disincentive to work.

These days, scientists usually bolster the second argument—the importance of teaching, rather than merely babysitting, young children—by talking about rapid brain growth in the first three years of life, when the critical developmental window for learning is wide open. The zero-to-three argument insists that these youngest children belong in an educational context and underscores their need for guidance and stimulation in addition to oversight.

But there may be no better illustration of the need or hunger for developmental help and constructive opportunities than the children who regularly try to climb the fence surrounding the Irma Hunter Wesley Child Development Center's playground. Inside the one-story building, the center is homey; its nursery is filled with wooden rocking chairs; a sunny library is decorated with stuffed animals and posters. There's even a tiny couch, where a toddler might curl up to read.

Outside the building, along a run-down stretch of Fort Lauderdale's Sistrunk Avenue, a bunch of neighborhood kids, ranging from four to about twelve, have none of these amenities. They don't even have a safe place of their own to play.

So they scale the fence daily with the hope of riding on the playground's swings and toy cars.

The sight of the littlest ones trying so hard and usually failing to get to toys pulls at the heartstrings. It's so easy to feel for the youngest ones—tiny ten-month-old Alexandria in the back of her mother's car or the babies left in their cribs at the Discovery Me Center. They so clearly are victims of a larger neglect. These kids can't even talk; how could they improve their lot? Yet, of course, even as they seemingly become better able to care for themselves, the older children are just as helpless. Capable of walking, running, and sometimes scaling a fence, the kids on Sistrunk Avenue are still losing the valiant struggle to keep themselves productively occupied.

The true heartbreak is that despite having reached the peak of their abilities, adults across the country have been just as powerless as the children in keeping young people safe and occupied when their parents work. And the failure is hurting not only Alexandria and the other tiny little ones. The rest of us are still waiting, too.

8

The Elusive Part-Time Solution

The Stay-at-Home Mom Crisis

It's easy to see how women wind up out of the workplace. Sometimes, a lack of maternity leave turns the birth of a child into an all-or-nothing proposition: leave the tiny baby before you're ready to or quit your job. Or, as we've just seen, the child-care options are so dismal, nothing feels right. And, of course, many women simply prefer to be with their children. But what's less obvious—or less talked about, anyway—is what happens to women once they do leave work. To whatever degree mothers who stay home choose to do so, they often find themselves in dire financial straits. Indeed, even as the image of the hyper-privileged opt-out mother lives on, recent census figures confirmed that stay-at-home moms tend to be less educated and poorer than the rest of mothers. So, instead of enjoying mommy-and-me yoga or relaxed walks in the park, too many are instead spend their time desperately searching for ways to earn money that allow them to continue caring for their children.

This is Rachel Foster's situation. With two girls, ages almost five and nine, she needs to be available for her daughters after school, but she also needs and wants to supplement the income of her husband, a truck driver who works nights. Ultimately, Foster, who lives in rural Kansas, would like to get her fifty-five-year-old husband, who has driven for more than thirty years, "off the road." He has knee problems and borderline diabetes, and Foster hates the thought of him behind the wheel all night long. Until she had surgery on her ankle about six months before I spoke with her, Foster had the perfect gig, working as a massage therapist around her daughters' schedules. But knowing she would soon be unable to work on her feet for long stretches, she began to look for another way to earn money shortly before the surgery.

It was around this time that Foster met another mother, Cindy, through a local online moms' group. "She was so sweet," Foster says of the woman who talked to her for an hour on the phone before signing her up with a company called Melaleuca. "She is so much more than my business partner, she's one of my best friends." Although the people who join Melaleuca often refer to the people who get them involved as mentors, there are several dimensions to their relationships. Every time Foster buys one of the company's four hundred household products, which include cosmetics and cleaning supplies, Cindy earns money. Cindy even earned money simply for getting Foster to sign up in the first place about five months back. Foster, in turn, has the same relationship to the ten people she's signed up in that time—all women and all of whom, like Foster, are obligated to buy a minimum amount of Melaleuca products each month (at least $50 worth). And so on down the line.

Foster is hopeful that she can eventually make $80,000 this way; indeed, the stay-at-home mom featured in a video on the company's Web site said she earned $90,000 in one year through Melaleuca. Yet in Foster's second and third months with the company, she didn't sign up any new customers, and, after factoring in the money she spent buying Melaleuca products, she lost rather than earned money. Cindy spent time on the phone with Foster afterward, helping her "work through" the loss, and suggested that Foster's mistake had been to devote too much of her time to helping the women she signed up with their own businesses. "I got into management mode, trying to help them," she explains.

The Internet, where Rachel Foster first met Cindy and searched for other part-time work opportunities, provides perhaps the best measure of the desperate need of many stay-at-home moms for part-time, flexible employment. Log on to the "I want to work at home!!!!" group (membership 82,408 at last count) in CafeMom.com, the largest social-networking site for mothers, and you can get a whiff of the despair. In one post, headed "desperatly [*sic*] need to be a WAHM," "Aiden's mommy" writes that she is looking for work because she, her husband, and their two-year-old can't afford to stay in their apartment. Anticipating that the family will have only $15 left by the end of the month, she notes that she can't afford to invest in a business. Thus, Aiden's mommy's post reads "no Avon."

A great number of these members are no doubt women whose earning potential is less than or about the same as what they would have to pay for child care. This situation is particularly common for women who have more than one child. A mother of two, for instance, might, depending on her children's ages and the local market rate for babysitting, have to pay in the neighborhood of $7 per hour for each child, or $14 per hour, and so would have to earn more than that per hour to make work out of the home worthwhile.

A vast, ugly free-for-all has sprung up to exploit mothers searching for flexibility and income. The Internet is so clogged with mom-targeted job scams, a recent Google search for "stay-at-home mother earning opportunity" was capped at fifteen million. Some companies, like Avon, require representatives to purchase merchandise that they'll theoretically sell at a profit to other mothers. Before Rachel Foster started her massage business, she spent a year working for Avon, during which she wound up making outlays for inventory, brochures, and travel, among other things, and losing $2,000.

Other companies require an up-front registration fee for members to gain access to exaggerated or nonexistent opportunities. Work-at-Home-Mothers' Web site (WAHM.com) posts an ad from FreelanceHomeWriters.com announcing the dire need for highly paid bloggers, who, according to the site, can make $61,440 per year—"Cha Ching!" Yet in order to tap into the supposedly gushing river of lucrative writing assignments, women have to fork over a $47 monthly membership fee.

According to Staffcentrix, a company that investigates some five thousand leads for such jobs every week, entities looking to make money from mothers themselves vastly outnumber real work opportunities online. For every legitimate work-from-home job advertised on the Web, there are some fifty-seven scams, according to Christine Durst, the cofounder and CEO of Staffcentrix. And that ratio doesn't include the spam that floods countless in-boxes daily.

Although one would think the reek of hucksterism would deter most job seekers, a startling array of ads announce these "job opportunities" with capital letters, exclamation points, dollar signs, and even, to convey the life of leisure you're supposed to live once you give them some money, palm trees. "Get Paid for Being a Mom!" "Your Own Crafts Business Making Photo Jewelry!" "Mom earns $250 in first week!" Many of the "jobs" involve selling everything from herbal energy drinks to mineral makeup, weight-loss powders, organic beef jerky, and Christian party kits, and often sellers have to purchase this merchandise first.

Perhaps because candles seem to suggest femininity and domesticity, these items loom especially large in the get-rich-quick—or get out-of-debt-quick—landscape. If you believe the ads, the road to riches is paved with wickless car and soy candles, flameless scented bars, sachets, and votives. Some mix of desperation and gullibility is the only possible explanation for the baffling idea that scented wax could be the solution to anyone's financial problems. Stay-at-home moms must be deep in a financial hole to believe they can "make money selling Christian candles" even while they sleep, as Christiannet.com promises, or to be moved to spend their precious dollars on candles by the Texas-based Scent-Sations' company, whose slogan is "Burn and Earn."

"The more desperate a demographic is, the more likely they are to be bamboozled by scams," says Durst, who has met dozens of women who have been burned by various scams in their search for part-time work. Staffcentrix contracts with the U.S. Army to help find legitimate part-time and work-at-home jobs for military wives (whose unemployment rate is upward of 20 percent, according to Durst), and many women approach her at workshops with their tales of woe.

Many of the scams she hears about are based on the multilevel-marketing model, like the one in which Rachel Foster has become ensnared. The disreputable multilevel-marketing companies are not unlike pyramid schemes, in that they are fraudulent plans that require an endless stream of new members. But in addition to having to recruit new dupes, participants in multilevel-marketing schemes such as Melaleuca, Herbalife, and Mary Kay also sell some sort of product. Hoping to distance themselves from both terms, such companies tend to refer to themselves as "direct sales" and give their recruiters fancy names like "Independent Beauty Consultants," as they're called at Mary Kay, or "Home Business Travel Agents," as they're called at the multilevel-marketing company YTB Travel.

The vast majority of the people who get caught up in multilevel-marketing schemes are women. (Eighty-eight percent of the people involved in direct sales in 2007 were women, according to the Direct Selling Association). And despite the big promises, most people, not surprisingly, are more likely to lose money than to get rich. According to the calculations of Jon M. Taylor, the director of Pyramid Scheme Alert and the author of *The Network Marketing Game*, only 0.13 percent of all Melaleuca participants earn a profit after their expenses and product purchases are taken into account.[1] (It would be difficult to earn enough to rival costs, which include a registration fee, mandatory monthly expenditures on products, purchase of the obligatory $199 "value pack" or $299 "career pack," and the cost of advertising to lure new customers.) Thus, according to Taylor, Rachel Foster's chance of winning with snake eyes at craps is about twenty-five times greater than her chance of succeeding as a Melaleuca distributor.

Many of these companies feed off—and, unfortunately, often wind up eroding—women's social networks. Rachel Foster found the women she's signed up—"my girls," she calls them—through her church, her daughters' friends' mothers, and ads on moms' Web sites. And the candle and makeup companies often encourage women to hold Tupperware-style parties to sell the products. Yet the pressure to exploit other women for their meager resources can end friendships, as it did for someone named Olivia, who posted on PinkTruth .org, a Web site for recovering Mary Kay conscripts. After her best friend recruited Olivia into the company, their relationship fell apart. Olivia describes Mary Kay meetings this way: "Inside, everyone was happy happy shiny sisterly love, etc. Outside, they huddled in packs, smoking cigarettes and ripping others apart with their nasty comments."[2]

There is ample evidence of women being bilked by blatantly fraudulent companies, but these cases are only very occasionally prosecuted. While state and federal laws prohibit pyramid schemes, many multilevel-marketing companies slither in the gray area between outright pyramid schemes and legitimate businesses, making them difficult to nail down and punish. The Federal Trade Commission (FTC) would be the likely agency to tackle the problem, but its efforts are hampered by a limited budget. According to Staffcentrix's Durst, who is assisting the FTC in an investigation of one predatory multilevel-marketing company, the agency can afford to go after only one of many people involved with the scheme, due to time and money constraints.

Although states tend to battle the same budget problems that the feds do, a few have sued multilevel marketers. In 2009, California had some success, suing and all but shutting down the state operations of YTB Travel, a company that reaches out to stay-at-home moms. (One of the company's Web sites features a bikini-clad woman on a beach with her laptop. There's even a "YTB nannies and moms" group on the Café Mom Web site.) According to papers filed by the California Attorney General's Office, which yielded $1 million in damages for the people of California, the company is a scam that "recruited tens of thousands of members with deceptive claims that members could earn huge sums of money through its online travel agencies." Of the 200,000-plus consumers who paid more than $1,000 over a year to operate YTB Web sites during 2007, 62 percent failed to earn a single travel commission.[3] According to its settlement with the attorney general, YTB can no longer issue travel credentials in California. But the company can still freely continue its operations in other states, of course.

In 2006, the Montana state auditor sued another multilevel-marketing company that promotes its business heavily to stay-at-home moms. Offering women "a business with no experience needed!" and "Huge quarterly bonuses!" Ameriplan could seem like a good solution to someone with a deep-enough need for both money and health insurance. Yet according to the suit, the company didn't actually hold up its end by contracting with local health care providers, leaving the Montanans who bought the company's "health discount cards" out of luck and their monthly fee, which ranges up to $59.95. Ameriplan gave the state $200,000 as part of a settlement of the suit, which charged the company with conducting a pyramid scheme, in addition to engaging in insurance and securities fraud.[4]

Ameriplan is significant not only for being a huge multi-level-marketing company that targets women. (Because it's "too much like a pyramid scheme," Staffcentrix's Durst puts Ameriplan in the scam category and won't allow it to post on her company's job boards.) The health-benefits company, as it calls itself, also provides a window into one of the reasons for many women's lack of decent flexible and part-time work options: our system of employer-based health insurance, which leaves so many women without coverage. Ameriplan not only capitalizes on the overall lack of health insurance nationwide (according to the company's Web site, the fact that seven in ten Americans are either uninsured or underinsured "presents the opportunity of a lifetime!"), it also particularly homes in on women's lack of health insurance.

Indeed, the lack of a health insurance system is intimately related to the employment difficulties among mothers. There's ample evidence that a growing number of full-time working mothers would prefer part-time work. A 2007 poll conducted by the Pew Research Center found that 60 percent of women who have children under eighteen and work full-time actually want to work part-time, up from 48 percent in 1997.[5] Only 21 percent of working women felt that full-time work was the ideal situation for them. (Perhaps this dissatisfaction shouldn't come as a surprise, given that the United States has the highest percentage of full-time working women of any country in the world.) While many of these women are working for the extra income, many, too, stay with their jobs because they have no other way to get health benefits for themselves and sometimes for the rest of their families.

Meanwhile, many stay-at-home mothers and part-time workers, of which most of the latter are women, remain uninsured. Even women who are pregnant and whose health has a direct and obvious bearing on fetal well-being don't necessarily get health insurance. In fact, throughout the country, it becomes harder, rather than easier, for women to get health insurance once they're pregnant. Thirty-eight-year-old yoga instructor and personal trainer Jemilla Mulvihill knows this firsthand. The near impossibility of getting private insurance was just one piece of bad news that Mulvihill received during her first few weeks of pregnancy. The other was that her boyfriend, with whom she had been planning to have a child, changed his mind about becoming a father. Almost immediately after Mulvihill announced the results of her home pregnancy test, he began to stay out all night drinking with his friends. When Mulvihill told him he'd have to get a job and help support the new addition, he said he'd rather kill himself.

Facing the prospect of supporting a child alone in New York City on her income of $30,000 a year, Mulvihill began to see the expenses ahead of her as obstacles to motherhood. It had been a stretch to cover rent and food even before she became pregnant. Afterward, both basics still loomed large, though not quite as large as the cost of health insurance, which she had done without up to this point. Being in good health and great shape, Mulvihill hadn't felt the need to spend scarce dollars on insurance before. When she had muscle aches, she'd get a massage. If she came down with a fever, she'd wait it out and hope for the best. This time, she knew, she wouldn't be able to get away with shortcuts. She was right. Even without the cost of prenatal care, an in-hospital delivery typically runs between $7,000 and $10,000, according to the March of Dimes Foundation.[6] Mulvihill knew that if anything went wrong, the costs could be way higher than that.

So she resigned herself to buying private insurance, even if she had to put it on her credit card and pay it off at some point in the distant future. A baby was far more important than a good credit rating. Yet after spending hours calling private insurance companies, she found that none would take her. The reason? Private insurers can legally reject pregnant women on the grounds that their pregnancy is a preexisting condition. Although federal law forbids group health plans from rejecting women for this reason, individual plans have no such restraint placed on them. Given the loophole, seemingly all private companies jump through it. Even though *not* getting prenatal care is technically a violation of the law (women could be prosecuted for neglect, though they rarely if ever are, according to family law experts), private insurance plans for individuals aren't required to help them get it.

Thus, pregnant women are regularly denied health insurance not in spite of their need for care but expressly because of it. Although some states loosen their Medicaid eligibility requirements for pregnant women, no state covers all pregnant women. So what's an uninsured pregnant woman to do if she can't afford insurance? Some women "spend down," forgoing income to qualify for Medicaid. Others take their chances. According to one study by the March of Dimes, 18 percent of uninsured pregnant women in 1996 went without needed medical care during the year in which they gave birth.[7]

For Mulvihill's part, she figured her options were to either find some crafty way to cover her medical costs or end the pregnancy. Luckily, the benefits worker she encountered granted her a Medicaid card, despite the fact that her income was slightly above the cut-off in New York City at the time. "I wanted to give her a hug," Mulvihill said later. "It was either have an abortion, or I'm going to have this child, and the decision was in this woman's hands."

Clearly, Pregnancy Insurance, the Texas-based Christian ministry that runs the Web site PregnancyInsurance.org, understands the dilemma. The site purports to offer solutions for uninsured pregnant women, heavily promoting two companies, Affordable Health Care Options (AHCO) and Ameriplan, neither of which, it turns out, actually offers insurance to pregnant women. (Other money-saving ideas for uninsured pregnant women offered on the site include signing up for Medicaid, eating well, and looking into home births, which are "considerably more economical than hospital births.")

As for AHCO, the company is not only not an insurance company, it's a blatant fraud that exploits pregnant women, according to the Texas office of the Attorney General, which sued AHCO in 2008, alleging that while the company sells a "Maternity Card" that it says offers maternity services, such as doctors' visits, hospital stays, lab work, sonograms, and prescriptions, "in truth and in fact the Maternity Card offers none of these services."[8]

When women realize they've been ripped off and try to get their money back (per the "ironclad guarantee" promised on the Web site), the company routinely refuses to do so, according to the suit. So much for the other pearl of wisdom offered by PregnancyInsurance.org: "Limit your amount of stress as much as possible."

Of course, Ameriplan, the multilevel-marketing company being sued for fraud by the state of Montana, is also unlikely to help women pay for either prenatal care or birth expenses. Yet while PregnancyInsurance.org purports to be independent and objective, the site, it turns out, is operated by a group that identifies itself as "a life-affirming Christian ministry" and that boosts both bogus insurance products, noting that it has "investigated" the companies through the Better Business Bureau and found them "to be in good standing." In truth, the Better Business Bureau gave both companies an "F" rating, logging 207 complaints against Ameriplan in the last year and a "significant number" against AHCO, some of which are "very serious," according to the bureau's site. When contacted, the manager of PregnancyInsurance.org acknowledged that AHCO had paid a referral fee to be listed but said that Ameriplan hadn't contributed any money to Pregnancy Insurance (and subsequently removed the information about the investigations into the companies' integrity).

Despite the sordid mess that has sprung from American women's intertwining needs for decent part-time work and health insurance, other countries have succeeded in ensuring women flexible work schedules. A big part of the solution is that all of these countries have universal health coverage, so that working fewer hours needn't mean losing the ability to get medical care. But the European Union has also clearly recognized the need for flexibility in work, having guaranteed parity in terms of pay and benefits for part-timers since 1997.[9] Germany and the United Kingdom have gone further, ensuring workers the right to request to change their hours.

But the clear leader in terms of flexible and part-time work options is the Netherlands.

With the satisfaction of family needs and desires in mind, the country has fastidiously created a "part-time economy" over the last few decades, passing and tightly enforcing laws that require employers to grant workers flexibility. While everyone has health insurance, regardless of his or her employment status, the Dutch have also passed a number of protections for part-time workers that allow men and women to make work fit into the rest of their lives, instead of the other way around. A 1982 agreement solidified the right to cut down work hours without sacrificing benefits.[10] And subsequent laws ensure that a worker's schedule can't be an issue in whether he or she has a contract extended or terminated.

Having harnessed the political will to make decent, well-paid, part-time jobs with good benefits available, the country now has the highest rate of part-time work in the world.[11] More than three-quarters of working Dutch women have part-time jobs—and not the low-paying, low-status type you find in the telemarketing/cashier/waitress ghetto where so many American mothers toil. (Multilevel-marketing schemes are few and far between in Holland, and companies masquerading as health insurance providers are nonexistent.) Essentially, Dutch citizens can tailor almost any job to a less than full-time schedule. Because nearly a quarter of working men (22.5 percent) also choose this part-time option, many Dutch couples have found a way for both parents to work and spend significant amounts of time with young children, and the country has taken an important step away from the overwork and overwhelm that define life in so many developed economies.[12]

. . .

The part-time protections in the Netherlands have been credited with raising women's employment—which, at 68 percent, is almost as high as the American rate—as well as boosting national fertility, because women are more open to having children if they can be moms while also maintaining their careers. Perhaps even more important, the Dutch model seems to offer women a measure of happiness and balance that's eluded most American women. As Ellen de Bruin, a journalist and the author of the 2007 book *Dutch Women Don't Get Depressed*, sees it, the key to Dutch women's contentment is freedom. (Ironically, in the United States, the same word, *freedom*, has come to mean the ability to succeed on one's own with minimal interference from government, while in the Netherlands the freedom to choose part-time work cited by de Bruin is the direct result of intensive government involvement in employment and family life.)

I met de Bruin in a restaurant at the iconic train station in Holland's capital, Amsterdam, and, for what it's worth, she did seem happy. Having ridden her bike to the station from her office in the middle of the afternoon (she works full-time as a newspaper reporter but largely sets her own schedule), she ticked off the various freedoms that she thinks are key to Dutch women's happiness, including the freedom to have children or not (a hefty 20 percent of Dutch women, including de Bruin, do not), to work or not, and, crucially, if they work, to set their own hours.

De Bruin was quick to admit there's something absurd about trying to quantify happiness. Do you measure endorphins? Count laughs? One Dutch professor, Ruut Veenhoven, whose findings were part of the fuel for her book, decided to ask people or at least to use survey data from around the world that asked participants to rank their happiness level on a scale of one to ten. According to the calculations of Veenhoven, a professor of social conditions for human happiness at Erasmus University in Rotterdam, the editor of the journal *Happiness Studies*, and the director of the online World Database of Happiness, Dutch women are the sixth happiest in the world. (The United States, birthplace of both "happy hour" and "the happy meal," ranks thirty-first in overall happiness, by the way. And Sweden, often thought of as the family-friendliest country in the world, is in eleventh place.)[13]

In their toy-filled apartment on the outskirts of Amsterdam, Nicolette Bunnik and her husband, Flor, are more concerned with the making of dinner than the pursuit of happiness, although, at least for the moment, the two are related. As the couple expertly juggles the tasks of setting the table and putting the finishing touches on bowls of chicken and vegetables, their sons, six-year-old Thomas and four-year-old Berend, play with trains on the kitchen floor. While the boys' sounds are largely playful ones, they escalate as the evening wears on, and by the time dinner is ready, everyone seems eager or perhaps happy to eat.

I went to the Netherlands hoping to get a sense of how spouses and partners who both work part-time operate. And, if the country falls short of being a domestic Eden, I witnessed more relaxed and pleasant family scenes there in one week than during the rest of my travels throughout the United States. Indeed, by American standards, Nicolette and Flor have a distinctly sane and egalitarian child-rearing routine. Neither one is locked into any parent-related task, be it making and packing lunches, dropping the boys at school, or bringing them home afterward. They both do all of these things, although who does what changes according to the weekday, because both Nicolette and Flor are home with the boys a fair amount. And the boys seem as excited to be with one parent as with the other.

A high school art teacher with shoulder-length blond hair, Nicolette now works 70 percent of full-time, putting in four days a week, three of them only from 9 a.m. to 3 p.m. Until two years ago, she worked half-time (because she is on an academic schedule, either way she is entitled to thirteen full weeks of paid vacation). Meanwhile, Flor, a tall man with salt-and-pepper hair, spends four days a week buying and selling construction equipment for a small Dutch company. In addition, his employer has agreed to accommodate a "calamity care" schedule, so he stays home when either of his sons is sick. Although Flor fears that his decision to go part-time may have limited his opportunities for advancement within the company, he's still pleased he made it and relishes the ample time he has to spend with his sons.

Even single mothers, for the most part, manage to work part-time and use child care sparingly. Take Fiona Huisman, a tall redheaded woman I met one afternoon in the small tree-lined city of Zaltbommel. Though she works only twenty-four hours per week at a fairly low-paying job, in which she counsels other single mothers, Fiona still manages to lead a relatively full and unharried life. Partly this is because she's careful to live within her means. Her top-floor walk-up apartment in a townhouse has plenty of room for her and her four-year-old son, Luca, but it's decidedly not luxurious, and Fiona has no car. Together with a subsidy that brings her child-care costs down to 30 Euros a month (about $42), these lifestyle choices allow Fiona a real life beyond work that is unimaginable to most American moms, single or coupled: she is actively pursuing her interest in dance, taking classes several times a week, regularly has coffee and movie dates with friends, and still spends as much time with her son as she likes.

Whether it's the cause or the by-product of their part-time economy, the Dutch clearly have different expectations about parenting and family. While 71 percent of toddlers spend some time in the publicly subsidized crèches, which are generally of better quality and more affordable than child care in the United States, parents there tend to eschew the idea of full-time or even near-full-time child care. Among the dozen or so part-time working parents I met in Holland, most sent their children to government-subsidized child care, or crèche, only two days a week. Even though the parents all held positive opinions of the crèche, no child spent more than three days a week there. With both parents working part-time schedules and often grandparents pitching in as well, a few days was all they needed. A recent study by Anmarie Widener, an expert on Dutch family policy, also found that the idea of leaving children in day care for an entire work week—as opposed to part-time —was anathema to Dutch men and women, with forty-nine out of forty-nine parents in her survey saying that three or four days of child care per week should be the maximum.[14]

And at least among the significant minority of parents who both have part-time schedules, there's a heavy emphasis on the involvement of fathers. "Sharing parenting happened quite easily," says Inge Houkes, a public health professor who lives in a suburb of the Dutch city Sittard. Inge works four days a week and spends one weekday at home taking care of her four-year-old daughter, Marit, and picking up her six-year-old, Britt, from school. Her husband, Olaf, an information technology worker in a large international firm, has exactly the same schedule, although he also stays home when either of the girls is sick. Both say that no negotiations or arguments preceded his decision to go part-time; they simply agreed that it made sense, and he requested the change from his employer. Because Inge's parents also spend one day with their granddaughters, Marit spends only two days in child care. And neither Inge nor Olaf feels particularly overwhelmed.

The Dutch system is by no means perfect. As Flor noted, some men feel that opting for part-time schedules limits their professional options. Some part-timers also find that it's harder to increase work hours from part-time back to a full-time schedule as their children grow, because employers aren't required to restore schedules back to their former, higher level after an initial reduction. Since her son turned four, Fiona, for instance, has wanted to increase her work hours but has been unable to do it. Some women have also criticized the part-time solution as perpetuating the power differential between men and women. Certainly, the Netherlands doesn't do as well as Sweden, for example, in terms of gender equity. Despite the fact that men and women have the same legal rights with regard to part-time schedules, women still make up the overwhelming majority of part-time workers, are responsible for more child care, and earn less than men do.[15]

Yet if Dutch women continue to shoulder most of the domestic burden, they are at least getting more help from their male partners than most American women do—and they have the time away from their legitimate, reasonable jobs in which to do their domestic tasks.

9
Baby Strike
The International Motherhood Experiment

Watching Dutch women in office attire pedal their children around on family-friendly bikes—presumably heading off to the crèche and then to their gratifying part-time jobs, or perhaps simply going home from work with the little ones for a fresh home-cooked meal—one can get the jealousy-inducing sense that Europeans have solved mothers' problems. But European countries, along with virtually every other privileged nation, have been struggling to adjust to the same overarching demographic and economic shifts facing the United States. In fact, these countries have one battle scar ours does not: dramatically plunging fertility. As women have gained access to jobs and education over the last forty years, they have had fewer children—a lot fewer. More than ninety nations throughout Europe and Asia now have fertility rates well below replacement level. (In both Macau and Hong Kong, the total fertility rate, the average number of children each woman has in her lifetime, dropped below one in 2008.)

In the United States, the total fertility rate has fallen, too, having dropped continuously for more than a century and a half up until 1975. Yet even as the nosedive has continued and gotten even steeper elsewhere, in the United States it's stagnated roughly at around 2.1 children per woman, or what's known as "replacement level," because it allows the population to hold exactly steady.

In the broadest sense, the decline in family size is not an entirely negative turn of events. Few women now want to have five children, which, for example, was the average in Italy around the turn of the century before its fertility rate began its steady decline to its current rate of 1.3. For a long stretch, the downward trend of birthrates paralleled the availability of reliable birth control, which is widely held as a positive development. Having fewer children made sense as families moved away from agrarian lifestyles, in which more hands to do farm work were a boon. And smaller families make less of a dent in natural resources.

Yet in many countries, the downward shift has continued to a point where it now threatens the supply of workers, soldiers, and payers into social-benefit systems. Some people are now predicting that given how far the Italian population has already contracted, it will be reduced to a third of its current size within forty years. But the downturn in fertility hasn't necessarily meant greater personal satisfaction. Finally freed from their lack of control over bearing too many children, a substantial number of women now feel that they're having too few.

Research in Western Europe shows that women typically say they want much bigger families than they have.

Often, the average number of children desired is around two, although, in fact, the average number of children that Western European women have in their lifetimes is around 1.4 per woman.[1]

Scholars blame the baby bust on several phenomena, including greater autonomy on the part of women, later marriages, and a drop in what one researcher calls "hopefulness about the future." Yet many now agree that at least part of the problem is due to the unpleasant and ultimately unsustainable pressure on women of doing both paid work and unpaid domestic work without having enough help. If becoming a mother requires a woman to take a huge financial and professional hit, the thinking goes, she will be far less likely to do it.

While the "international baby strike" has imperiled the future economies of entire continents, it's also yielded some fascinating discoveries. Spurred by the prospect of less productive, graying populations, policy makers have begun to explore the connection between the decision to have children and the generosity of policies that allow women to continue working after having them. The results of this "motherhood experiment" are promising: just as obstacles to simultaneously holding a job and raising children can deter women from becoming mothers, it seems that programs that ease women's ability to do both can nudge them toward having bigger families. Take the Netherlands, for instance. Around the time that the first part-time work protections were passed, Dutch women had a historic low average birthrate in their lifetimes of 1.47 children per woman. Although it's impossible to tease out the precise role the part-time regulations played, the fertility rate has steadily crept upward since that time, reaching 1.66 in 2009.[2]

The capacity of public policy to influence reproductive decisions is so well accepted that at least forty-five countries in Europe and Asia have programs aimed at either maintaining or raising their fertility rates, many of which are based on facilitating a woman's ability to work. A clear lesson is emerging from these efforts: that the right public supports can increase both the number of children that people have and women's participation in the workforce.

It may come as no surprise to working mothers that the two policies that seem to have the most consistently positive effect on fertility rates are the availability of flextime work and good, affordable child care—both of which allow women to have children without forfeiting their income and professional accomplishments, although with somewhat different results.

How do we know these programs work? While some policies appear to have an effect in certain countries and not in others, researchers have begun to document the positive impact of certain advances on both the number of children that women have and women's overall participation in the workforce. One study of child benefits in eighteen countries, for instance, calculated that a 10 percent increase in child-benefit levels translated into a 25 percent increase in women's fertility.[3] In Norway, the effect of increased access to child care on local fertility levels has been measured, with women becoming mothers earlier if they live in towns that have more child-care slots available. As the percentage of children in child care in a small geographic area increases from 0 to 75, the probability of a twenty- to twenty-four-year-old bearing a child rises from 4.9 percent to 11 percent; for a twenty-five- to twenty-nine-year-old, the figure rises from 10.4 percent to 14 percent.[4] The timing of births turns out to be key, because the drop in the fertility rate is tied to the fact that many women inadvertently delay getting pregnant until it's no longer biologically possible.

The generosity of paid parental leave, which in many countries is available to men as well as women, is also thought to affect birthrates in certain places. Some policy analysts have linked an upswing in the Swedish fertility rate to the government's expansion of guaranteed paid parental leave from nine to twelve months in the late 1980s. Similarly, cuts in benefits there shortly afterward were blamed for a downturn in the birthrate. In France, which now has the highest birthrate in Europe, women who have a third child receive discounts on trains and public transportation, as well as on subsidized, high-quality child care, and about $1,200 in cash.

Accommodating working mothers isn't a new idea, of course. As we'll see in the next chapter, some other countries began instituting paid maternity leave one hundred years ago. And there's also a long history of using public policy to increase childbearing—some of it morally repugnant. The governments of Hitler and Mussolini both attempted to force people, or rather certain people, to have children. Mussolini's government levied a special tax on bachelors. And in the 1980s, Singapore introduced a series of measures to encourage its better-educated citizens to start families, while at the same time discouraging poor and less-educated women from doing the same. Defenders of the campaign described it as an effort to improve the "quality" of the population.

This latest wave of pronatalist policies is more likely to be justified as an expedient way to offset the population decline, which, ironically, has been steepest in countries, mostly Catholic, that have long been associated with big families and traditional values. Portugal, Spain, Italy, and Greece, where the classic "male breadwinner" family model still holds strong, now have among the lowest fertility rates in Western Europe. Meanwhile, countries that support high numbers of working women, such as Finland, Norway, and Denmark, have among the highest birthrates.[5]

How did what's been called the "fertility paradox" come about? One explanation is a gap between family-oriented values and the entry of women into the workforce within these more traditional countries, which demographic theorist Peter McDonald refers to as a "public policy dissonance."[6] Women there now have greater access to education and jobs, as they do elsewhere in the developed world. Yet family is still typically seen as the responsibility of individuals rather than the government, so there is little public support to help working mothers. Thus, women in these "male breadwinner" countries are more likely to perceive their options as either to work *or* to have children, rather than do both. And their participation in the workforce and their fertility both tend to be lower.

Several countries are leading the charge to ease this paralyzing burden. As Maria Nistor, the Romanian immigrant who was fired for taking the day off to be with her sick daughter, knows, formerly communist countries in Europe have had relatively high levels of child care, paid leave, and women's employment for decades. Although some have taken backward steps as they've transitioned to democracy, in many cases, these countries have been able to build on these existing services. Meanwhile, the European Union has raised the floor on support for working parents in all member countries by mandating minimum standards for work hours, paid holidays, and family leave.

In terms of child care, one of the two crucial ingredients contributing to women's combined productivity and reproductivity, Belgium and France have helped lead the way, instituting public, universal child-care programs that enroll 99 percent of three-, four-, and five-year-old children of working parents in the country.[7] Sweden, which enrolls 82 percent of toddlers in its public child-care program, also shines among other family-friendly countries for its child-care successes.

Indeed, Sweden has come to be the family-policy yardstick against which most countries look at least somewhat pathetic. Back-to-back with the United States, the Nordic Eden, which spends about twice what we do on social programs as a portion of gross domestic product, looks something like Wilt Chamberlain. In the interest of fairness, it's worth noting that the entire population of the prosperous Scandinavian nation is roughly the size of New York City's. And its tax rate is considerably higher. Still, the Swedes reap copious enviable benefits from their public investment. In addition to Sweden's national child-care system being used by the vast majority of families, the country offers family leave that covers up to eighteen months off at partial pay; a guarantee that parents can work reduced hours until their children are eight; sixty days of paid leave each year a parent can use to care for a sick child; and a "leisure-time care" program, in which children receive before- and after-school care until age twelve, with sliding-scale fees. Oh, yes, then there's the "daddy leave," an additional four weeks of paid nontransferable time that fathers can take off to spend with their infants—one of several government attempts to encourage men's involvement in child rearing.

Indeed, Sweden's biggest achievement may be its empowerment of women. With equal TV time for women's and men's sports, an almost perfect gender divide in its parliament, and a cabinet-level minister for gender equality, Sweden was named the third most advanced country on the globe in terms of gender equality by the World Economic Forum in 2008 (the United States, by the way, ranked twenty-seventh, just behind Barbados).[8] While maintaining a relatively high fertility rate for Europe, 1.85, Sweden also has among the highest rates of female workforce participation. Family supports, especially child care, have made this possible by alleviating responsibilities on the home front, so that women can rival men in both their earnings and time spent working.

In terms of employment, the United States and the Netherlands have many similarities. Both countries have comparable female employment rates and, along with countries such as Finland, France, and Belgium, comparable numbers of couples in which both parents work. What makes the United States different is that because we have the highest rate of women doing full-time work in the world, in many of these dual-income couples both parents work very long hours. And yet our fertility remains relatively high, so women are often combining motherhood with inflexible full-time workloads. While most Dutch women work part-time and sometimes get the help of partners with similarly flexible schedules, most American women work grueling schedules with little relief from other helping hands.

Perhaps the biggest consequence of this dubious international distinction is that the constant stresses of working and caring for children leave many American mothers not only miserable, as we've seen, but also depressed. The elevated stress levels most American women face compared to their counterparts in other rich countries may help explain not only our relatively low "happiness" scores, but also our relatively high depression rates. About 17 percent of Americans are depressed at some point in their lives, as opposed to 3 percent of people in Japan, for example, according to the most recent cross-national comparison of depression rates, conducted by psychiatric epidemiologist Myrna Weissman in 1996.[9] In all countries studied, women's depression rates were roughly twice as high as men's. Interestingly, the disease typically sets in when women are in their early to mid-twenties, around the time they're likely grappling with the incompatibility of their competing responsibilities. Several studies have also shown that single moms here have roughly twice the depression rates of married ones, which makes sense when you consider the hefty burden they shoulder by themselves.

Although having a "little bundle of joy" is generally expected to brighten your life, recent research has shown that at least in the United States, parenthood tends to be a downer, with both male and female parents being more depressed than their childless peers.[10] It's not marriage or even working that gets to them—both having a partner and being employed are boons to mental health, according to Robin Simon, a sociologist at Florida State University who has focused on the prevalence and causes of parents' depression. But add the burden of children and parents report more feelings of sadness, loneliness, restlessness, fear, and anger. Perhaps not surprisingly, parents who live with their minor children report less frequent feelings of calm and contentment. As with nonparents, about twice the number of women who have kids are depressed compared to their male partners, regardless of racial or ethnic background or economic status.

Although no international studies have yet compared parents' depression rates, Simon thinks the parent-depression connection may be unique to—or at least particularly extreme in—the United States because of our distinctly unsupportive family context. The financial and time stresses that define parenthood in this country are "far from ideal for allowing them to reap the full emotional benefits of having children," says Simon. As she sees it, the social conditions in which Americans parent may, in terms of mental health, at least, cancel out the inherent emotional rewards of having children.

Which brings us to the mystery of American fertility. Why, if child rearing under our particular circumstances is so difficult that it often leads to depression, do Americans continue to have as many children as we do? In many ways, the United States is like the "male breadwinner" countries now experiencing baby droughts. With a majority of women who expect—and are expected—to join the workforce and few good options in terms of child care or flextime work (fewer, indeed, than most of the European countries that are experiencing plunging fertility rates), the United States would seem to have a classic case of the public policy dissonance that Peter McDonald describes. Yet we continue to have babies.

Part of the explanation for our high fertility rate is found in Mississippi and certain other poor spots around the country, where limited access to birth control and abortion contributes to high rates of unplanned pregnancies and births. Less control over fertility tends to mean more kids. (The average number of children born to a woman in Mississippi is 2.3, for instance, compared to 1.7 in Vermont.)[11] Another part of the phenomenon can be explained by the high numbers of Latinos immigrating to the United States, who, on average, have more children than do non-Hispanic white and black Americans. (The Hispanic fertility rate was 2.3, according to 2006 census numbers, compared to 1.8 for non-Hispanic whites.) Still another puzzle piece is our particularly American aversion to talking about—and teaching kids about—sex, which has in turn contributed to our extraordinarily high teen pregnancy rate. The U.S. teen pregnancy rate, for instance, is more than ten times higher than the Dutch one.

Whatever the exact mix of reasons behind our persistently high fertility rate, it's clear that without a drop in family size or any major accommodations from the government and employers, something else had to give. Because the international data suggest that no population can sustain double duty of paid work and domestic responsibilities, unaided, you'd expect a contraction in some other area of American women's lives. It's in this context that we might revisit David Cotter's mysteriously flattening and down-turning graph lines. While Sweden's gracious family policies were fostering near gender equity in that country, our failure to ease women's dual roles seems to have manifested in the pullback from public life that Cotter and his colleagues documented. In this view, the exodus of some women from the workforce, the dip in their earnings, and the slowing of their forays into male-dominated professions suggest that women finally burned out on doing both caretaking and earning without enough help.

There's no other obvious explanation for women's paralysis, no single event to tie to the phenomenon. Instead, it's like water that's heated very slowly to a boil: the combined burden of work and family had been bearable up to a point and then simply wasn't anymore. The seemingly abrupt halting of women's ascent is, in this view, a correction, a delayed but inevitable expression of the fact that women simply can't do everything without an infrastructure to support them. It's not unlike the housing bubble—or the bursting of it. Just as more and more families became unable to pay their mortgages, more and more women began to reckon with their own untenable work-life realities.

If the housing bubble formed around our fantasy that everyone could afford his or her own home, economic reality be damned, the bubble of women's progress grew around delusions of gender equity. We've been patting ourselves on the back for having so many women in the workplace, despite the fact that we haven't instituted the laws and the policies to keep pace with these changes and to make women's lives livable.

Without the kinds of support found in many other countries, Americans have become international outliers in terms of not only fertility, but also the duress of their daily lives. Public programs designed to lighten their burden could no doubt change that, as they have affected the daily lives—and subsequently, the reproductive decisions—of others throughout the world. There's no reason to think that American women won't be just as easily influenced by family-friendly services and policies as women throughout the rest of the world. Although there's little expectation that real help could raise women's workforce participation and fertility rates, which are already among the highest in the developed world, there's clearly plenty of room for innovations to boost women's spirits and quality of life.

10

The Blame Game

How and Why We Wound Up in Last Place

When I saw *Sicko*, Michael Moore's documentary about the American health-care system, the audience tsk-tsked at the sight of insurance executives and groaned at the gross parts, as you might expect. But the loudest expressions of shock and disgust were elicited not by severed fingers, but by a smiling postpartum doula, who arrived to help out a new mom with laundry and cooking, courtesy of the French government. It was as if Freddy Krueger had shown up, detergent in hand. "No way!" shouted a scandalized woman a couple of rows ahead of me. Perhaps she had had less help after she gave birth? If so, watching the doula scene apparently brought up the most primal of feelings: jealousy. Like a hungry toddler forced to watch her best friend wolf a cupcake, my fellow viewer clearly wanted what should have been hers—and was stunned by the unfairness of not getting it.

Even Moore, who had an ample supply of health-related outrages at his disposal, clearly saw the contrast between the American and French approaches to family support as so galling and surprising as to warrant taking his movie a little off-topic. Indeed, the notion of government-subsidized household help was a central laugh-cry line in *Sicko*, with Moore, in typical Moore fashion, bringing his own dirty clothes to a federal building and, as part of the movie promotion, offering his personal laundry services to a "randomly selected Republican."

How did we get so far out of step with the rest of the developed world that the sight of other governments supporting families elicits gasps of shock and howls of envy—and the notion of our country doing the same is met with belly laughs (or at least bitter chuckles)? Why have we as a nation remained so ignorant of the way other countries treat their families that the fact of government-issued family support amounts to an unimaginable plot twist? And exactly how out of step are we, really?

To get a good grasp on this last question, consider that the United States chose not to sign on to an International Labor Organization (ILO) agreement, supported by at least thirty-three countries, which said that female workers should get cash benefits in addition to twelve weeks of job-protected leave around childbirth. Consider, then, that the ILO maternity convention in question took place in 1919, when the Model-T was just switching over from crank to electric starter and before "talkies" replaced silent films.[1]

The decision not to sign on to the ILO convention can be seen as a critical fork in the road between the paths of the

United States and other developed countries, with ours leading toward the current American scattershot nonsystem of family support and the other path heading toward the more comprehensive approaches of most other rich nations. The differences between Europe and the United States have long held true for most social-welfare issues, including health care and income support, but, to continue with the example of paid maternity leave, it's worth noting that we've not only failed to get it during this vast stretch of years but even, in some ways, moved further from the possibility of paid leave since that fork in the road.

Back then, there was at least hopefulness about the possibility of instituting nationwide support for women workers after the birth of a child. Other countries were doing it. Why not us? But early advocates of leave seem to have gotten bogged down in details. A faction within the American Association for Labor Legislation pushed to include a call for "maternity insurance" in a 1915 proposal, for instance, but because of an internal dispute over who exactly should be covered, the final report wound up omitting it.[2] Other early proponents of maternity benefits got tripped up by whether they should insist that protections for pregnant workers be part of national health coverage (which, sadly, they seemed to think was also imminent). And the political prospects for paid leave seemed to only grow dimmer over the years.

Meanwhile, some other countries had already established leave policies well before the 1919 agreement. Germany adopted its maternity leave law in 1883, Sweden in 1891. In France, female teachers and postal workers got maternity leave in 1910.[3] By 1919, the year of the ILO convention, six countries had instituted job-protected maternity leaves and nine offered at least some pay along with time off. Although a number of early leave policies were unpaid and didn't offer job protection, even these offered the fundamental recognition that women's paid work should accommodate the reality of reproduction.

No one knew then just how far the American path would ultimately stray from the other, much better worn, one. The same year that the maternity convention was signed, the chief of the U.S. Children's Bureau of the Department of Labor, a woman named Julia Lathrop, issued a report on international maternity leave policy, in which she wagged a scornful finger at the United States, referring to it as "one of the few great countries which as yet have no system of State or national assistance in maternity."[4] You can almost hear Lathrop, who was known as "America's first official mother," clucking her tongue in consternation. How could a country as rich and fantastic as hers be so out of step? Almost a century later, with more than 120 countries around the world now providing paid maternity leave, the question lives on.

Families' needs have only expanded since the days of Julia Lathrop and the demand for services has grown. According to a 2007 survey undertaken by the National Partnership for Women & Families, a majority of both male and female respondents—regardless of age, race, income, education, or parental status—support paid leave.[5] Public support for increasing access to preschool and after-school programs is also high, even among economic developers and employers. Not surprisingly, interest in government spending on child care and early education is highest among young parents, with 85 percent of all men and women between eighteen and twenty-nine favoring government-funded child care for working parents, according to a 2008 survey conducted by the Rockefeller Foundation and *Time* magazine.[6] And while there has been less legislative attention to the matter of part-time work, a majority of employed women have clearly announced their desire for flexible options. So why, even though most Americans want these supports, which are necessary to secure their foothold in the workforce—and, sometimes, to maintain their sanity, as well—are American families still without them?

For the answer, it helps to look back to what earlier lawmakers must have considered solutions to work-family dilemmas. To the extent that the U.S. government attempted to address family issues, it has offered limited benefits only to certain groups, rather than taking a universal approach, and the patchwork has never come close to covering everyone who needed covering. When it was available at all, family support was distributed to subgroups of women, often separated by race and income. "Mothers' pensions," the state-run forerunners of welfare that began in the early 1900s, for example, provided financial help to some single women. But in the first few decades of the twentieth century, the overwhelming majority of mothers' pensions went to white women whose husbands had died or abandoned them, as historian and legal scholar Dorothy Roberts detailed in her book *Killing the Black Body*. In 1935, black people were more explicitly excluded when mothers' pensions went on to become codified with the Social Security Act.[7]

Many of the later programs that sprang up to support American mothers and families, such as cash benefits, child-care assistance, and subsidized preschool education, were "means-tested," or restricted only to the neediest, and have remained both underfunded and politically tainted by their association with the poor. When it came to family support, more often than not, the government preferred to issue nonmandatory recommendations, rather than requirements, leaving employers, churches, and charities to fill in the gaps. On the positive side, the private sector did much to fulfill families' desperate needs, providing nurseries and help to struggling families with housing, food, and income. On the negative side, the assistance given by these groups fell short of meeting the true need, while making it easier for the government to view the work-family problem as solved.

With a policy vacuum at the federal level, family-related issues often fell to the states. Yet for the first several decades after the ILO convention, the handful of states that took on the issue of workers giving birth simply required them not to work, without addressing job security or helping make up for the lost income. The only federal law that addressed the issue, the Maternity and Infancy Act of 1921, expressly forbade mothers from receiving any money to replace lost earnings.[8] While the ban on wage replacement likely discouraged some women from joining the workforce, as its authors no doubt hoped it would, it also meant that some less fortunate women were not only working, but also working right before and after birth out of financial necessity.

Now, with near gender parity (at least in terms of sheer numbers) in the workplace, it's hard to imagine why women didn't push harder to get accommodations like flextime, maternity leave, and affordable child care. Although women clearly wouldn't have chosen our nonsystem, they did have a role in allowing it to evolve. Special protections were in some ways a casualty of many feminists' laser focus on equality. First- and second-wave feminists generally felt that their gains were too precarious, their determination to ascend from the pit of sex discrimination too great, to draw attention to anything maternal. So they often prioritized equal treatment, such as the ability to get paid the same amount as men for the same work, over accommodations that could be seen as special treatments, such as the ability to take time off from that work if necessary.

There simply wasn't room for nuance in the push for equality.

To be fair to those early feminists, their circumstances demanded it. It's worth remembering that throughout much of the last century and a half, American women were systematically excluded from many aspects of public life, often on the grounds that money, work, and power were inconsistent with their family responsibilities. The laws and policies that did this were in keeping with an explicit national belief that women belonged at home. As the U.S. Supreme Court justices wrote in an 1873 decision that upheld Illinois's refusal to let a woman practice law: "The natural and proper timidity and delicacy which belongs to the female sex evidently unfits it for many of the occupations of civil life."[9]

Quaint and outdated as this idea may sound now, government protections for this "fairer, weaker" sex persisted well into the twentieth century, as laws remained on the books depriving women of such basic rights as owning property, retaining their surnames after marriage, and being hired and paid based on merit. Feminists' primary goal of eliminating such discrimination sometimes conflicted directly with the fight for accommodations for caretakers on the job—or at least seemed to. So, when legislation that limited the number of hours women could work was introduced in the 1930s, for instance, the National Woman's Party and the National Federation of Business and Professional Women opposed it on the grounds that it was part of a male effort to limit female competition in the workplace.[10] Similarly, in the early 1970s, feminists challenged school board policies because they required, rather than simply allowed, pregnant teachers to take maternity leaves for several months before and after birth.

It wasn't all women's fault, of course. The nation's geographic isolation contributed to our relatively spotty approach to helping families. At least early on, physical distance seems to have kept Americans from comparing our policies more directly with those of European nations, most of which seemed to collectively nudge one another along through the years and ultimately came to share in the European Union's ability to set minimum policy standards. (With oodles of information about various countries' approaches to these problems now easily available with the click of a mouse, perhaps the real reason for the ongoing ignorance about the relative stinginess of American family policy—and the shock value of the doula scene in *Sicko*—is that most working parents in the United States can't bear to think much about how and why life is easier for families in other countries.)

Sheer luck and circumstance also bear some of the blame. There were several missed opportunities, like the one in 1919. History seemed to intervene at key points when advocates might have succeeded in getting family-friendly measures passed. In 1942, as women flooded the workforce during World War II, the Women's Bureau of the Department of Labor recommended that working women get six weeks of prenatal leave, as well as two months following childbirth. The federal government also funded child-care centers across the nation to facilitate women's work. But when the war ended and men returned home to reclaim their jobs, the push toward maternity leave and the federal funding of child care quickly fizzled out. Then, while dipping fertility rates in Europe sparked interest in policies that eased women's burdens on that continent, the United States underwent a baby boom, which meant there was no similar pressure to prod the debate further here. (Indeed, the vast policy differences between the United States and Europe are testament to the large role that population concerns played in pushing Europe to accommodate women workers.) Later, Jimmy Carter came into office brimming with ideas about how the government might help families, but by then, the oil crisis had drained money from social spending, and his "Nine Point Family Plan," which included a call for federally funded child care, went unheeded.[11]

Unfortunately for those who were hoping for more public support for working women and families, fate did seem to smile on Ronald Reagan, whose landslide election in 1980 can be seen in part as a reaction to increased social spending on social security, disability insurance, and welfare. Benefiting from both charisma and timing, Reagan managed to establish himself as the moral arbiter of family values, while at the same time slowing and sometimes halting progress toward policies that would actually help families. With a one-two punch, combining a laissez faire approach to business with Christian "pro-family" rhetoric, Reagan essentially squelched the possibility of increasing government support for families for decades to come. As he framed it in a 1986 "radio address to the nation on Family Values," the family and the feds were enemies, with the American family having "lost authority to government rule writers."[12]

Reagan was tapping into a deep national well of conservatism, which celebrates self-reliance and, conversely, frowns on anything that gives off even the faintest whiff of dependence. Well before anyone was smearing Barack Obama as a socialist (indeed, well before Barack Obama was born), taunting along those lines helped keep proposed public family supports from becoming realities. Back in the 1940s and 1950s, publicly funded child care was decried as "communistic" and "un-American." In 1975, conservative columnist James Kilpatrick railed against legislation that would have funded child care, among other services, as the "Sovietization of the American family."[13] And throughout her career, Phyllis Schlafly has slung mud at a long list of work-life balance proponents, accusing them of everything from endorsing socialism to promoting "feminist pork."[14]

Reagan simply tweaked that message, bringing—and, more important, leaving in his wake—an extreme traditionalism toward government's relationship with families that was all but inoculated from criticism by the religious and "pro-family" rhetoric he combined with it. By the logic of the Reagan era, which coincided with the rise of the Moral Majority and other traditional "family values" groups on the religious right, publicly funded programs, such as paid leave and subsidized child care, were seen as threatening intrusions not only to business, but to families as well. Spending government money to foster women's independence was a potential threat to morality and the nuclear family. Religious right groups were so successful in drumming up support for conservative "values issues," such as abortion, that they sometimes entirely subsumed women's issues. (One measure of the religious right's success on this front is that some conservative lawmakers who had opposed maternity leave were ultimately won over to the idea after being convinced that job-protected time off from work would help bring down the abortion rate. For them, abortion had become politically potent enough to trump the worry that leave would solidify women's place in the workforce.)

In retrospect, the verbal and political assault on anything that might be seen as supporting working women should have been expected from Reagan and fellow conservatives, who were serving and opining just as women were transitioning into paid work. Because the shift was still under way, they arguably still had hope of reversing it. In 1980, when Reagan was first elected, the number of women in the workforce had just passed the 50 percent mark. He and his like-minded colleagues correctly saw the country at a sort of tipping point. Clearly, by not extending family supports that would help women push further into work, they hoped to put the genie back in the bottle and force a return to traditionalism.

Although the point at which anyone could reasonably argue that women could or should leave the workforce has long passed, and Reagan along with it, "family values" lives on as boiled-down political-speak for conservative, religious beliefs and opposition to abortion. Republicans succeeded in identifying themselves with the term as recently as 2004, with 80 percent of voters who listed "moral values" as their most important issue in a CNN exit poll voting for a second term for George W. Bush. Indeed, Reagan's legacy—the political right's claim on the term "family values" and its link with opposition to programs supporting working women—has enjoyed a bizarre longevity, limiting or outright prohibiting virtually every legislative attempt to institute work-family accommodations between his administration and the current one.

What little money the federal government spent on child care in that time was allocated in the context of welfare, and support for it was marshaled on the grounds that it promoted self-sufficiency (which, in the case of poor women, seems to have outweighed the value otherwise placed on mothers' traditional roles). Meanwhile, as Europe was instituting protections for part-time work, the few such efforts here were tarred as unfair to employers, and none passed. And opposition from social conservatives and business groups severely limited the political possibilities of maternity leave. Although there was broad support for paid maternity leave when Clinton came into office, the Family and Medical Leave Act that he signed was so shrunken from its original form that some leave proponents didn't even consider it a victory. Earlier versions would have given all workers twenty-six weeks for medical leave and eighteen for parental leave, both with pay, yet the law that passed in 1993 granted only twelve weeks off, unpaid, and covered about 60 percent of workers.[15]

Any significant success that work-family advocates have had since then was achieved at the state level. Yet there, too, family-friendly measures have faced tough opposition. Although a few states managed to pass paid leave laws, each success was hard-won, as business leaders and, to a lesser degree, social conservatives have made fighting such legislation a priority. Even though paid leave costs employers nothing or next-to-nothing in the states in which it now exists (wage replacement comes from a statewide insurance fund, in most cases), the business community has continued to insist that it places a mandate on employers that strangles free enterprise.

Over the decades, this tactic has worn down and cowed even some of the most determined supporters of paid leave, who are understandably leery of asking, or even hoping, for too much. So, legislative proposals tend to start small and wind up even smaller, if they pass at all. In the successful campaign for paid leave in New Jersey, for example, advocates only briefly discussed the possibility of asking for more than twelve weeks for workers to care for sick family members or parents to bond with an infant. Because the federal family leave law only provided that amount of time off, "there was no point in asking for more," according to Karen White, the director of the Working Families Program at the Center for Women and Work and an advocate for paid leave who was very involved in the effort.

The lawmakers who sponsored New Jersey's paid leave bill were similarly pessimistic, or perhaps just realistic, about their prospects, so much so that they scaled down their measure even before there was any public complaint about demanding too much paid time off. While the initial legislation called for workers to get twelve paid weeks off for a medical emergency or time to bond with an infant, the bill's sponsors fairly quickly lowered the amount to ten weeks and soon afterward to six. "It was almost like, well, they'll never go for twelve weeks, so we'll just bring it down ourselves," says White, who described the bill's supporters as "just arguing with themselves." The state law that ultimately passed in late 2007 provided six weeks of partially paid leave.

State lawmakers with family-friendly inclinations had good reason to expect the worst. Across the country, business groups racked up a string of victories against efforts to pass paid leave. By the time the New Jersey paid leave law finally passed in 2007, similar proposals had been knocking around the state legislature for almost ten years. None had gotten past the local chamber of commerce, the New Jersey Business and Industry Association, and other business groups, which argued that paid leave interfered with business owners and would be vulnerable to abuse by employees. Meanwhile, at the same time that state legislators were fighting over paid time off, the Bush administration was working to scale back the already anemic national unpaid leave law on the federal level, attempting to narrow the medical conditions that qualified for time off and decrease the minimum amount of leave an employee could take.

One can only imagine the level of horror the pioneering Julia Lathrop might feel were she to rise from her grave and find the United States still without paid maternity leave. If she thought her beloved country was a laggard ninety years ago, today she'd no doubt decide that because of its colossal failure to pass a national paid leave law and countless other forms of support for working families, it was no longer quite so great. A few state-level paid leave laws would probably be of little solace.

Indeed, it's hard to get too excited about the incremental progress we've made so far. None of the paid leave laws that have passed in California, Washington, or New Jersey provides more than six weeks off or two-thirds of the salary they're replacing. (In Washington, the benefit is just $250 per week.) Getting a fraction of your salary for a handful of weeks after you have a baby or a family medical emergency is still a far cry from having months off at full or near-full pay or, for that matter, having the government pay someone to do your laundry and tuck a homemade lasagna away in your freezer. But it's clearly a step in the right direction, a sign that the political logjam around family support may be beginning to break.

The upside of waiting almost a century for a political victory—or a partial one—is that there's plenty of time to contemplate our failures, which have included earlier attempts to push for maternity leave solely on behalf of mothers, as opposed to family and medical leave for all workers. That lesson first became clear in 1984, when a California court struck down that state's new maternity leave law, ruling that it discriminated against men. Since then, state-level solutions have encompassed medical leave for both men and women, which can involve caring not only for one's children, but also for other close relatives and even oneself. Because these laws benefit more people, paid leave has escaped its ghetto and become a workers' issue, rather than merely a women's issue. And because the coalitions behind such laws are broader, they have a better chance of passing. But the biggest boon to women is that these non–gender specific leave laws allow for at least the possibility that male partners will take time off, and that future supports will also give both men and women the flexibility to tackle a combination of paid and domestic work.

Our latest economic troubles offer their own silver lining, in the form of increasingly desperate human need that, with luck, might snap the United States out of its decades of inaction around family policy. Even back in the Reagan era, many women fell into the considerable gap between having an income low enough to qualify for means-tested programs and having enough money to comfortably eschew a paycheck. Now, with the economic crisis bearing down on everyone, the notion that the goodwill of employers and a combination of programs for the poorest women will solve our nation's family problems has gone from highly unrealistic to laughable.

Dismaying as it may be to weigh our grueling reality against family life in the rest of the world, now is clearly the time to do it. And once we truly appreciate how much less supportive the United States is of its families and how much easier life could be, we'll surely take the steps to make it so. Really appreciating the scope and horror of casualties from the War on Moms leaves us no choice but to act. Rather than simply drooling over everyone else's goodies, we'll just have to find a way to finally get our own damn cupcake.

Epilogue

The writing of this book took longer than expected, in part because I had two children myself during the process. As a result, many of the people I've spoken with have moved on in notable ways since I first met and wrote about them. I've followed up with a few of them here.

Just after her second birthday, Bethanie Gartner, Devorah's daughter, learned to walk. Given that she began toddling about a year later than most, it would have been easy to see the delay as a disappointment. But, since Bethanie lagged even further behind when she was learning to eat, drink, and sit, her ability to walk at all struck her mother more as a miracle and even more as the fruit of almost two years of painstaking effort by Devorah, Bob, and a small army of physical therapists. A year after that major leap forward, Bethanie learned to run. "I remember the autumn day when she saw me and flung out her arms and ran toward me," Gartner recalled recently. "She looked totally normal in that moment."

In many ways, Bethanie Gartner *is* normal. Now nine, she is an energetic child whose braids and spirit bring to mind Pippi Longstocking. Bethanie prefers Harry Potter, however, and, having read the entire series, she can chat at length about her favorite characters and plot twists. When she's not reading, she might be cooking or helping her mother with the little kids in the child-care center that Devorah now runs for the Gartners' Upstate New York synagogue.

Physically, Bethanie has come further than anyone—except, perhaps, her parents—expected she would. After lagging in almost every physical measure, she can now do cartwheels, propel herself along the monkey bars, pass the deep-water test, and even tap dance (or at least take a tap-dancing class, in which she is neither the best nor the worst student). She does have some lasting limitations from the stroke she suffered before she was born. A litany of likely lifelong problems with her balance, digestion, muscle tone, heart, visual processing, and hearing keep her and her parents traveling a regular circuit of specialists.

Because of lasting cognitive problems, Bethanie has been classified as a disabled student. It's particularly hard for her to remember lists of things, such as tasks she has to accomplish before going to school, which means that getting ready to leave the house often takes her quite a while. Every day, it's as if she has to put on socks and shoes, gather her school books and coat, and shut out the lights for the very first time. Like most mothers, Devorah Gartner sometimes finds her child's foibles trying. Though, most probably don't experience the flush of relief, which Devorah Gartner still feels regularly, that she's had the chance to raise her bouncy and sometimes frustrating nine-year-old.

The Gartners' continuing push forward, uphill though it may be, is almost enough to qualify for a happy ending. But the financial part of their story doesn't wrap up quite as neatly. Now that Devorah is working full-time for the synagogue, she once again has a steady, if modest, income, and the family is certainly more stable than it once was. Because her employers are understanding about her daughter's ongoing medical needs, Devorah also has the flexibility she still often requires. Though she frequently puts in more than forty hours a week, when Bethanie gets sick, Devorah is almost always able to take care of her. And when Devorah's parents fell ill a few years ago, she had no difficulty getting the time off to move her father, who had had a stroke, into her house while her mother was in the hospital.

Yet, the Gartners' ordeal took a lasting financial toll. They are still paying off the debt they incurred in Bethanie's first years of life. The digging out process has been slowed by the fact that the family's out-of-pocket medical costs exceeded $5,000 last year alone. (Insurance foots only part of the bill for Bethanie's medications and specialists.) Meanwhile, the couple's devastated credit rating has yet to pull out of the D range. Never having returned to the corporate world, Devorah now earns about half of what she did nine years ago and even less of what she might have wound up earning had she been able to stay on her career path. With a salary of $48,000, Bob has become the primary bread winner and continues to provide the family with health insurance. Unfortunately, he has to commute six hours a day (three hours each way) to do so. And recently Devorah's already modest income has become less reliable as the financial crisis took its toll on the synagogue's child-care center. Because a considerable number of families can't keep up with payments, Gartner has had to forego her paycheck on more than one occasion.

In New Mexico, Kalen and Carissa Lopez finished their allotted year in the at-home-infant-care program, which meant that Kalen had to return to work. The transition was rough on both mother and baby. And the difficulty was compounded—or at least given another layer of absurdity—by the fact that the work Kalen was returning to was in a day-care center. These days, she drops her one-year-old off with her mother-in-law so that she can go take care of other people's one-year-olds. Since she earns only $800 monthly (up from $600 when she started) and pays her mother-in-law $450, the elaborate switcheroo is all so that she can bring home between $150 and $350 a month.

Four months into the arrangement, Carissa still screams at the top of her lungs each day as they approach the door of her grandmother's house. Kalen has better impulse control, as you'd expect, but she too is frustrated by the situation. As she heads off to work to watch the toddlers at the center learn to talk and jump and drink from cups, she often wishes she could spend more of her time watching her own daughter do the same things. Still, Kalen is resigned to being back at the center—and to the fact that she'll likely have to continue working there for a while. Unexpectedly pregnant with a fourth child (she had thought it was impossible to get pregnant while nursing), Kalen will only be able to stay home with the newest little one for six weeks. At that point, her maternity leave will end and mother and baby—along with toddler Carissa—will all spend their days at the day-care center. Kalen will be able to go into the next room to nurse her new little one during breaks, though only for the first four months, according to the center's policy. After that, she expects she'll just "get used to missing her."

Down in Florida, after a year on the waiting list, little baby Alexandria did get a child-care subsidy, which freed her mother, Denise, from having to either cobble together last-minute arrangements or bring her daughter to work. Unfortunately, there was no space available for Alexandria at the center where her older siblings attend an after-school program, so after work, Denise first picks up the older children at one center and then drives to another fifteen minutes away to pick up Alexandria.

When I was trying to catch up with Glabedys, the Florida mother who was living off donated food so she could afford to send her daughter to day care, I heard a tale that seemed to perfectly sum up the chaos that marks the lives of so many low-income moms. I was unable to actually speak with Glabedys because she didn't have a phone and had left her job at the factory where I had previously reached her. But, in the process of trying to track her down, I did reach Pamela Hollingsworth, the director of the Busy Bees Preschool in Broward County, which Glabedys's daughter, Valerie, had attended. Hollingsworth reported that Glabedys had stopped bringing Valerie to preschool unexpectedly some months after I had met her, leaving behind an unpaid tuition bill of several thousand dollars. Unbeknownst to Hollingsworth, Glabedys had struck a deal with one of the school's teachers, giving the woman her car in exchange for the teacher's promise to pay her daughter's tuition. The teacher, however, made only one payment. With an unemployed husband and a newborn daughter of her own, she, too, was having money troubles. Though she was staying late after full days of teaching to earn money cleaning the classroom (despite having given birth just weeks before), she was unable to keep up with the tuition. Soon after she stopped paying, Valerie and Glabedys disappeared.

Hollingsworth says late and altogether unpaid tuition bills, always a commonplace of running a child-care center, now occur far more frequently as the economy has unraveled in the past year and a half. Glabedys's particular situation highlights the layered nature of the crisis, with teachers and parents often in essentially the same sinking ship. Indeed, many directors of child-care businesses are little better off. Because of the center's falling income, Hollingsworth has had to take on a full-time job to make ends meet, even while she continues to fulfill her full-time responsibilities as the director of her center. Linda Carmona Sanchez, who directs the A-Plus Early Learning Center in Miami, has also taken on a second full-time job. Both Hollingsworth and Sanchez report coming into their centers at odd hours—sometimes as early as four o'clock in the morning—to do paperwork, make sure there's milk in the fridge, and otherwise prepare for the school day, before starting their other workday.

For her part, Angela, the mom we met briefly in the introduction, is undergoing her own transition. When I first met her, she was on maternity leave, fretting over whether to return to work in the human resources department of a large bank. Though she had worked part-time for two years before going on leave, the bank eliminated that option while she was home with her newborn. After much deliberation, Angela decided to go back to work full-time. But her return lasted only a single day, at the end of which she was reduced to tears. Her decision to quit stemmed both from not wanting to spend fifty hours a week away from her children and from the chilly reception she got upon her return to the bank. Though she feels she was essentially pushed out of her job, when she called a hotline set up for people with family-related discrimination problems, she was told that she didn't have grounds for a suit. So Angela and her husband, who works freelance in the restaurant industry, are struggling to cover expenses—including health insurance for Angela and the two children—with only his income.

While families across the country carry on with their own shifts and struggles, the most important change that's taken place nationwide is a political one. With a swing-set behind it and dozens of parents of young children working within, the White House is now more receptive to family issues than it's been in years. President Obama, the father of two school-aged girls who was himself raised by a single, working mother, clearly understands that structural problems make life extremely rough for working families and for women in particular. Already, his administration has made steps toward fixing some of these issues. Hopefully, the long overdue—if incomplete—overhaul of health care will be only the first act. Vice President Joe Biden's middle-class task force, with one of its main goals "improving work and family balance," suggests that issues like paid sick leave, paid maternity leave, and a real system of affordable, quality child care may also soon see the light of day. Meanwhile, with groups such as the Partnership for Women and Families,

Momsrising, and Legal Momentum preparing to pounce on this rare political moment, the War on Moms is beginning to feel less one-sided. Indeed, this low historical moment may offer the opportunity we've long awaited, with just enough dissatisfaction and suffering to fuel the change we need.

But, if in fact we're hearing the first rumblings of change, a full-fledged counterinsurgency is still far off. Even as the foundering economy has made many of the problems facing families worse, some lawmakers have worried about spending our much-depleted public funds to "bail out" American families. As we wait to see whether this potential turning point will be squandered like previous ones, the gap between us and the rest of the developed world should remind us that, even if it's hard to scrape up the money to move forward, we can't afford not to do it.

As of this writing, there are countries where a child's illness need not bring the risk of financial ruin for the parents. There are countries where having a child is not likely to end or stunt a woman's career. There are countries where good education for children younger than five is as available as education for those over five. There are countries where women needn't choose between barely seeing their family and barely getting by. And there are countries where public policies—and not just scolding voices—tell women it's important to spend time with newborn children. Yet, still, the United States is not among them.

Notes

1. Falling

1. U.S. Department of Health and Human Services. Indicators of Welfare Dependence. Washington, DC: DHHS, 1998.
2. Sara R. Collins, Jennifer L. Kriss, Michelle M. Doty, and Sheila D. Rustgi, "Losing Ground: How the Loss of Adequate Health Insurance Is Burdening Working Families," *Commonwealth Fund Report*, vol. 99 (2008).
3. Steven Ruggles, Matthew Sobek, Trent Alexander, Catherine A. Fitch, Ronald Goeken, Patricia Kelly Hall, Miriam King, and Chad Ronnander, "Occupational Segregation: IPUMS 25-54, Employed, 1950–2000," *Integrated Public Use Microdata Series: Version 4.0* (machine-readable database) (Minneapolis: Minnesota Population Center [producer and distributor], 2008).
4. 2000 U.S. Census.
5. Ruggles, et al., "Occupational Segregation: IPUMS 25-54, Employed, 1950–2000."
6. Rutgers Center for American Women and Politics, "Levels of Office: Congress," 2009.

7. Rutgers Center for American Women and Politics, "Women in State Legislative Elections 1976–2008."
8. Rutgers Center for American Women and Politics, "Statewide Elective Office," 2009.
9. Census Bureau reports and data, *Current Population Reports, Median Earning of Workers 15 Years Old and Over by Work Experience and Sex*, 2009.
10. National Committee on Pay Equity, "The Wage Gap Over Time: In Real Dollars, Women See a Continuing Gap," September 2009, available at http://www.pay-equity.org/info-time.html.
11. Rebecca M. Blank, "Women and Economic Recovery" (paper presented at the Institute for Women's Policy Research's Achieving Equity for Women symposium, Washington, D.C., April 2, 2009).
12. Joan C. Williams, "Hitting the Maternal Wall," *Academe* 90 (2004): 16.
13. Bureau of Labor Statistics.
14. Sharon R. Cohany and Emy Sok, "Trends in Labor Force Participation of Married Mothers of Infants," *Monthly Labor Review* (February 2007).
15. David Cotter, Joan Hermsen, and Reeve Vanneman, "A Stalled Revolution? Gender and Work in the 1990s," paper presented at the annual meeting of the American Sociological Association, San Francisco, CA, August 14, 2004. Also see David Cotter, Joan Hermsen, and Reeve Vanneman, "The End of the U.S. Gender Revolution: Changing Attitudes from 1974 to 2004," paper presented at the annual meeting of the American Sociological Association, Montreal, Quebec, Canada, August 11, 2006.
16. Lisa Belkin, "The New Gender Gap," *New York Times Magazine*, September 30, 2009.

2. Supermom Returns

1. Lisa Belkin, "The Opt-Out Revolution," *New York Times Magazine*, October 26, 2003.
2. Joan C. Williams, Jessica Manvell, and Stephanie Bornstein, "'Opt Out' or Pushed Out? How the Press Covers Work-Family Conflict: The Untold Story of Why Women Leave the Workforce,"

report by the Center for WorkLife Law, University of California, Hastings College of the Law, 2006.

3. Phyllis Schlafly, *The Power of the Positive Woman* (New Rochelle, N.Y.: Arlington House, 1977), 49.
4. Linda Hirshman, "Homeward Bound," *The American Prospect* (November 2005).
5. *Lopez v. Bimbo Bakeries USA, Inc.*, Superior Court, San Francisco County, California (May 27, 2007).
6. *Lust v. Sealy, Inc.*, 277 F. Supp. 2d 973 (W.D. Wis., 2003), aff'd, 383 F.3d 580 (7th Cir., 2004).
7. *Walsh v. National Computer Systems, Inc.*, 332 F.3d 1150 (8th Cir., 2003).
8. *Knussman v. State of Maryland*, 272 F.3d 625 (4th Cir., 2001).
9. 2007 Sleep in America Poll, National Sleep Foundation.

3. 'Til Dishes Do Us Part

1. Suzanne M. Bianchi, John J. Robinson, and Melissa A. Milkie, "No Time for Their Kids? Working Parents and Time with Children," research and clinical notes presented at the Tenth Anniversary Conference of the Council on Contemporary Families, the University of Chicago, May 4–5, 2007.
2. Pew Research Center, "Modern Marriage: I Like Hugs. I Like Kisses. But What I Really Love Is Help with the Dishes," July 18, 2007, http://pewresearch.org/pubs/542/modern-marriage.
3. Francine Deutsch, *Halving It All: How Equally Shared Parenting Works* (Cambridge, MA: Harvard University Press, 1999); University of Michigan Institute for Social Research, Panel Study of Income Dynamics, 1968–Present.
4. Michigan Institute for Social Research, 2008.
5. Ellen Galinsky, James T. Bond, Lois Backon, Erin Brownfield, and Kelly Sakai, "Overwork in America: When the Way We Work Becomes Too Much, Families and Work Institute, March 2005.
6. Joshua Coleman, "Good Reasons for Men to Do Housework: Happier Marriages, Better Kids," research and clinical notes presented at the Tenth Anniversary Conference of the Council on Contemporary Families, the University of Chicago, May 4–5, 2007.

7. Michelle L. Frisco and Kristi Williams, "Perceived Housework Equity, Marital Happiness, and Divorce in Dual-Earner Households" *Journal of Family Issues* 24 (2003): 51.
8. Joshua Coleman, "Parents Need to Get Out of the House Sometimes!" paper prepared for the 11th Annual Conference of the Council on Contemporary Families, the University of Illinois–Chicago, April 25–26, 2008.
9. Ritesh Mistry, Gregory D. Stevens, Harvinder Sareen, Roberto De Vogli, and Neal Halfon, "Parenting-Related Stressors and Self-Reported Mental Health of Mothers with Young Children,"*American Journal of Public Health* 97 (2007): 1261.
10. Shannon N. Davis, Theodore N. Greenstein, and Jennifer P. Gerteisen Marks, "Effects of Union Type on Division of Household Labor: Do Cohabiting Men Really Perform More Housework?" *Journal of Family Issues* 28 (2007): 1246–1272.
11. Elizabeth Warren and Amelia Warren Tyagi, *The Two Income Trap: Why Middle-Class Mothers and Fathers Are Going Broke* (New York: Basic Books, 2003).
12. 2007 American Psychological Association Survey, *Stress in America*.
13. Janet C. Gornick, "The Government's Gone Fishin': The Absence of Work/Family Reconciliation Policy in the United States," research prepared for the Council on Contemporary Families Symposium: Who Cares? Dilemmas of Work and Family in the 21st Century, Chicago, Illinois, October 20, 2006.
14. Rebecca Ray and John Schmitt, "No-Vacation Nation," Center for Economic Policy Research, May 2007.
15. According to a 2007 AFL-CIO survey. This difference can be accounted for by the increased likelihood that women hold part-time and low-wage jobs, both of which are less likely to come with paid vacations.
16. Ray and Schmitt, "No-Vacation Nation."
17. Jared Bernstein, *Crunch: Why Do I Feel So Squeezed?* (San Francisco: Berrett-Koehler, 2008).
18. Suzanne Bianchi, Vanessa Wight, and Sara Raley, "Maternal Employment and Family Caregiving: Rethinking Time with Children in the ATUS," paper prepared for the ATUS Early Results Conference, Bethesda, Maryland, December 9, 2005.

19. Charlotte J. Patterson, "Family Relationships of Lesbians and Gay Men," *Journal of Marriage and Family* (March 2004): 1052–1069.
20. Christopher Carrington, "Domesticity and the Political Economy of Lesbigay Families," in N. Gerstel, D. Clawson, and R. Zussman, eds., *Families at Work: Expanding the Bounds* (Nashville, TN: Vanderbilt University Press, 2002).
21. Department of Labor figures.
22. Harriet B. Presser, "Employment Schedules among Dual-Earner Spouses and the Division of Household Labor by Gender," *American Sociological Review* 59 (1994): 348.
23. *Chris Schultz v. Advocate Health and Hospitals Corporation, et al.*, No. 01 C 702 (N.D. Ill., 2002).

4. The Problems We Wish We Had

1. Leslie Bennetts, *The Feminine Mistake: Are We Giving Up Too Much?* (New York: Voice, 2007).
2. Allison Pearson, *I Don't Know How She Does It: The Life of Kate Reddy, Working Mother* (New York: Anchor Books, 2002).
3. Judith Warner, *Perfect Madness: Motherhood in the Age of Anxiety* (New York: Riverhead Books, 2002), 21.
4. Lisa Belkin, "The Pushmipullyu of the Life-Work Conflict," Life's Work, *New York Times*, November 5, 2006.
5. Pamela Stone, *Opting Out? Why Women Really Quit Careers and Head Home* (Berkeley: University of California Press, 2007), 195.
6. *Catalyst: 2008 Catalyst Census of Women Board Directors in the Fortune 500*, 2009.
7. Sylvia Ann Hewlett, *Creating a Life: Professional Women and the Quest for Children* (New York: Hyperion, 2002). According to Hewlett, 49 percent of mid-career women who made $100,000 a year or more were childless, compared to only 10 percent of men.
8. Jody Heymann, *The Widening Gap: Why America's Working Families Are in Jeopardy and What Can Be Done about It* (New York: Basic Books, 2000).
9. Sylvia Ann Hewlett: *Off Ramps and On Ramps: Keeping Talented Women on the Road to Success* (Boston: Harvard Business School Publishing, 2007).

10. Jeff Doran and Nina Cole, "Becoming a Contact Center Employer of Labor Marketplace," *Customer Relationship Management* (June 2004).
11. Center for American Progress, April 25, 2008.
12. Elizabeth Warren and Amelia Warren Tyagi, *The Two-Income Trap: Why Middle Class Mothers and Fathers Are Going Broke* (New York: Basic Books, 2003).
13. Allen J. Fishbein and Patrick Woodall, "Women Are Prime Targets for Subprime Lending," *Consumer Federation of America* (2006).
14. Steven Greenhouse, *The Big Squeeze: Tough Times for the American Worker* (New York: Alfred A. Knopf, 2008).
15. Gregory Acs, Katherine Ross Philips, and Daniel McKenzie, "Playing by the Rules, but Losing the Game: Americans in Low-Income Working Families," in Richard Kavis and Marc S. Miller, eds., *Low-Wage Workers in the New Economy* (Washington, D.C.: Urban Institute Press, 2001), 21–44.
16. Elizabeth Lower-Basch, "Opportunity at Work: Improving Job Quality," Center for Law and Social Policy, *Opportunity at Work Series*, Paper No. 1 (2007).
17. Economic Research Service, "Food Security in the United States," U.S. Department of Agriculture (November 2008).
18. Barbara Duffield and Philip Lovell, "The Economic Crisis Hits Home: The Unfolding Increase in Child and Youth Homelessness," National Association for the Education of Homeless Children and Youth (December 2008).
19. As Barbara Ehrenreich spelled out in her June 13, 2009, op-ed piece in the *New York Times*, "Too Poor to Make the News," the "already poor, the estimated 20 percent to 30 percent of the population who struggle to get by in the best of times," are largely missing from media coverage of the economy.

5. Testing the Bootstraps

1. Children's Defense Fund.
2. Mississippi State Department of Health, Public Health Statistics, IMR by County 1998–2007, produced November 2,

2008, available at http://www.omhrc.gov/Assets/pdf/Checked/1/dimemime.pdf

3. *National Vital Statistics Reports*, vol. 57, no. 14, Centers for Disease Control and Prevention, April 2009.
4. Lawrence B. Finer et al., "Timing of Steps and Reasons for Delays in Obtaining Abortions in the United States," *Contraception* 74, no. 4 (2006): 334–344.
5. Ted Joyce and Robert Kastner, "The Impact of Mississippi's Mandatory Delay Law on the Timing of Abortion,"*Family Planning Perspectives* 32, no. 1 (January–February, 2000).
6. Mark Nord, Margaret Andrews, and Steven Carlson, *Household Food Security in the United States*, USDA, 2006.
7. Center on Budget and Policy Priorities' analysis of 2007 Census Bureau data.
8. Jean Reith Schroedel, "Is the Fetus a Person? A Comparison of Policies across the Fifty States," *Theoretical Medicine and Bioethics* (October 29, 2004): 385–389.
9. Cynthia E. Miree and Irene Hanson Frieze, "Children and Careers: A Longitudinal Study of the Impact of Young Children on Critical Career Outcomes of MBAs,"*Sex Roles: A Journal of Research* (1999).
10. Ann Crittenden, *The Price of Motherhood: Why the Most Important Job in the World Is Still the Least Valued* (New York: Henry Holt, 2001).
11. Mark Lino and Andrea Carlson, "Expenditures on Children by Families, 2008." U.S. Department of Agriculture, Center for Nutrition Policy and Promotion, 2009. Miscellaneous Publication no. 1528–2008.
12. Mississippi Department of Education, *Mississippi Student Information System Classroom Teachers Report*, May 28, 2009.
13. Leonard M. Lopoo, "Fertility Trends, Maternal Characteristics, and Poverty in the American South,"*Insights on Southern Poverty* 4, no. 1 (2006): 8–10.
14. *2006 American Community Survey*, U.S. Census Bureau.
15. *Making the Grade on Women's Health: A National and State-by-State Report Card 2007*, National Women's Law Center,

Washington, D.C.; Misha Werschkul and Erica Williams, *The 2004 National Overview Report: The Status of Women in the States*, Amy Caiazza and April Shaw, eds., a report by the Institute for Women's Policy Research, November 2004.

16. *Fertility, Family Planning, and Reproductive Health of U.S. Women: Data from the 2002 National Survey of Family Growth*, Vital and Health Statistics, Series 23, Number 25, Centers for Disease Control and Prevention, and National Center for Health Statistics, December 2005.
17. G. Ryan, et al., "A Majority of Women Delay Childbearing in Both Fertile and Infertile Groups despite Understanding the Risks of Aging on Fertility," *Fertility and Sterility* 84, issue null (September 2005): S73-S73.

6. Congratulations, Now Back to Work

1. 2002 census.
2. Jody Heymann, Alison Earle, and Jeffrey Hayes, "The 2007 Work, Family and Equity Index: How Does the United States Measure Up?" Institute for Health and Social Policy, Project on Global Working Families, Montreal, Quebec; Boston, MA.
3. U.S. Department of Labor (2000), appendix A-2.
4. Bureau of Labor survey, U.S. Department of Labor, *Balancing the Needs of Families and Employees: Family and Medical Leave Surveys*, 2000.
5. *Maternity Leave in the United States: Paid Parental Leave Is Still Not Standard, Even among the Best U.S. Employers*, IWPR #A131, Institute for Women's Policy Research, August 2007.
6. 2007 Department of Labor figures.
7. *Maternity Leave in the United States*, IWPR #A131, August 2007.
8. *2008 National Study of Employees*, Families and Work Institute.
9. Heymann, Earle, and Hayes, "The 2007 Work, Family and Equity Index: How Does the United States Measure Up?"
10. M. Eberhard-Gran, and others, "Postnatal Care in a Cross-Cultural and Historical Perspective," *Tidsskr Nor Laegeforen* 123, no. 24 (December 23, 2003): 3553–3556.

11. Pinka Chatterji and Sara Markowitz, *Family Leave after Childbirth and the Health of New Mothers*, NBER Working Papers 14156, National Bureau of Economic Research, Inc., 2008.
12. Elizabeth C. Hair, et al., "Early Return to Work, Long Work Hours, and Maternal Depression: Lessons from the Early Childhood Longitudinal Study, Birth Cohort 2001," APPAM Fall Conference, Child Trends, November 3, 2006.

7. Good Day Care Is Hard to Find

1. Jennifer Mezey, Mark Greenberg, and Rachel Schumacher, *The Vast Majority of Federally-Eligible Children Did Not Receive Child Care Assistance in FY 2000: Increased Child Care Funding Needed to Help More Families*, Center for Law and Social Policy, revised 2002.
2. Between 2000 and 2007, the number of children receiving help has fallen, while the number of children living in low-income families potentially eligible for assistance has grown, according to Danielle Ewen of the Center for Law and Social Policy. As a result, the share of unserved children today is likely larger than it was in 2000.
3. Hanna Matthews, *Child Care Assistance Helps Families Work: A Review of the Effects of Subsidy Receipt on Employment*, Center for Law and Social Policy, April 2006.
4. Karen Schulman and Helen Blank, "State Child Care Assistance Policies 2008: Too Little Progress for Children and Families," issue brief, National Women's Law Center, September 2008.
5. Fight Crime: Invest in Kids, *High Quality Pre-Kindergarten Can Prevent Teenage Pregnancy and Future Crime in Tennessee* (Nashville, TN: Fight Crime: Invest in Kids, 2006).
6. Pre-K Now, "New York State Profile 2008," http://www.preknow.org/resource/profiles/newyork.cfm.
7. NACCRRA, *Parents and the High Price of Childcare: 2009 Update*, Arlington, Virginia: NACCRRA, 2009.
8. Janet C. Gornick, *The Government's Gone Fishin': The Absence of Work/Family Reconciliation Policy in the United States*, paper

presented at the Work Family Dilemma: A Better Balance, New York, February 2, 2007.

8. The Elusive Part-Time Solution

1. Jon M. Taylor, "Some Shocking Statistics: Comparing Recruiting MLM's with No-Product Pyramid Schemes, and with Gambling," Consumer Awareness Institute (2009), http://www.mlm-thetruth.com/ShockingMLMstats.htm.
2. Pink Truth, "Consultant Stories: Olivia,"http://www.pinktruth.com/index.php?option=com_content&task=view&id=960&Itemid=21.
3. *People of the State of California v. YOURTRAVELBIZ.COM, aka YTB.COM*, complaint for permanent injunction, civil penalties, restitution, and other equitable relief (August 2008).
4. Montana State Auditor's Office, "Morrison Announces $200,000 Settlement with Ameriplan to Resolve Fraud Allegations," October 24, 2006.
5. Pew Research Center, *Fewer Mothers Prefer Full-Time Work* (Washington, DC: Pew Research Center, July 2007).
6. March of Dimes, *The Healthcare Costs of Having a Baby* (White Plains, NY: March of Dimes, 2007).
7. Amy B. Bernstein, "Insurance Status and Use of Health Services by Pregnant Women," AlphaCenter, prepared for the March of Dimes, 1999, http://www.marchofdimes.com/files/bernstein_paper.pdf.
8. *State of Texas v. Brian James McDonald; Aaron Christopher Bouren; AHCO Direct, LLC; AHCO Agent, LTD; and AHCO Contract Servicing, LTD; D/BA/ Maternity Card and Affordable Healthcare Options*, Plaintiff's Original Petition (April 14, 2008).
9. The Council of the European Union, *COUNCIL DIRECTIVE: 97/81/EC of 15 December 1997 concerning the Framework Agreement on Part-Time Work Concluded by UNICE, CEEP and the ETUC* (Brussels: The Council of the European Union, 1997).
10. Wim van Oorschot, *The Dutch Welfare State: From Collective Solidarity toward Individual Responsibility*, Centre for

Comparative Welfare Studies, Working Paper no. 2006-41, Department of Economics, Politics and Public Administration, Aalborg University, 2006.

11. Jon C. Messenger, "Working Time at the Enterprise Level: Business Objectives, Firms' Practices and Workers' Preferences," in *Working Time and Workers' Preferences in Industrialized Countries: Finding the Balance*, ed. Jon C. Messenger (New York: Routledge, 2004).
12. Anmarie J. Widener, "Doing It Together: Mothers and Fathers Integrate Employment with Family Life in the Netherlands," in *Reconciling Family and Work: New Challenges for European Social Policies*, ed. G. Rossi (Milano: FrancoAngeli, 2006), 162–182.
13. Ruut Veenhoven, *World Database of Happiness*, Erasmus University Rotterdam, http://worlddatabaseofhappiness.eur.nl.
14. Widener, "Doing It Together," 162–182; Anmarie Widener, "Sharing the Caring: State, Family and Gender Equality in Parental Leave Policy," unpublished dissertation, 2006.
15. Ibid.

9. Baby Strike

1. John Bongaarts, "Fertility and Reproductive Preferences in Post-Transitional Societies," in *Global Fertility Transition*, Rodolfo A. Bulatao and John B. Casterline, eds. (New York: Population Council, 2001). While there's some evidence that at least in German-speaking countries, the average number of children that women say they want is beginning to drop as far down as 1.7, it's still higher than the number of children they actually have.
2. Central Intelligence Agency, *The CIA World Factbook* (Washington, DC: Central Intelligence Agency, 2009), https://www.cia.gov/library/publications/the-world-factbook/rankorder/2127rank.html.
3. Francis G. Castles, "The World Turned Upside Down: Below Replacement Fertility, Changing Preferences and Family-Friendly Public Policy in 21 OECD Countries," *Journal of European Social Policy* 13 (2003): 209–227.

4. Ronald R. Rindfuss, et al., “Child Care Availability and First-Birth Timing in Norway,”*Demography* 44 (2007): 345–372.
5. Gianpierro Dalla Zuanna and Guiseppe A. Micheli, eds., *Strong Families and Low Fertility: A Paradox? New Perspectives in Interpreting Contemporary Family and Reproductive Behaviour* (Dordrecht, The Netherlands: Kluwer Academic Publishers, 2004), 7.
6. Peter McDonald, “Gender Equity, Social Institutions and the Future of Fertility,”*Journal of Population Research* 17 (2000): 1–16.
7. Janet C. Gornick, and Marcia K. Meyers. “Supporting a Dual-Earner/Dual-Carer Society” in Jody Heymann and Christopher Beem, eds., *Unfinished Work: Building Equality and Democracy in an Era of Working Families* (New York: The New Press, 2005), 371–408.
8. Ricardo Hausmann, Laura D. Tyson, and Saadia Zahidi, “Global Gender Gap Report 2008,” World Economic Forum, 2008.
9. Myrna Weissman, et al., “Cross-National Epidemiology of Major Depression and Bipolar Disorder,”*JAMA* 276 (1996): 293–299.
10. Robin Simon and Ranae J. Evenson, “Clarifying the Relationship between Parenthood and Depression,” *Journal of Health and Social Behavior* 46 (2005): 341–358.
11. U.S. Department of Health and Human Services, *National Vital Statistics, CDC* (Washington, DC: U.S. Department of Health and Human Services, 2009).

10. The Blame Game

1. Steven K. Wisensale, *Family Leave Policy: The Political Economy of Work and Family in America* (Armonk, NY: M. E. Sharpe, 2001).
2. The American Association for Labor Legislation, *The American Labor Legislation Review* (New York: The American Association for Labor Legislation, 1917).
3. Wisensale, *Family Leave Policy*.
4. Dulcie Straughan, “Women’s Work: Public Relations Efforts of the U.S. Children’s Bureau to Reduce Infant and Maternal

Mortality, 1912–1921,"*Public Relations Review* 27 (2001): 337–351.
5. Lake Research Partners for the National Partnership for Women and Families, *Key Findings from Nationwide Poll on Paid Family and Medical Leave* (Washington, DC: Lake Research Partners for the National Partnership for Women and Families, 2007).
6. The Rockefeller Foundation, *Time Campaign for American Workers Survey* (New York: Rockefeller Foundation, 2008).
7. Dorothy Roberts, *Killing the Black Body: Race, Reproduction, and the Meaning of Liberty* (New York: Pantheon, 1997).
8. Elisabetta Vezzosi, "Why Is There No Maternity Leave in the United States?: European Models for a Law That Was Never Passed," paper presented at the 19th Annual Conference of the Research Committee on Poverty, Welfare, and Social Policy, Northwestern University, Chicago, IL, September 8–10, 2005.
9. Irene Padavic and Barbara F. Reskin, *Women and Men at Work*, 2nd ed. (Thousand Oaks, CA: Pine Forge Press, 2002).
10. Jo Freeman, "From Suffrage to Women's Liberation," in *Women: A Feminist Perspective*, 5th ed., Jo Freeman, ed. (Mountain View, CA: Mayfield, 1995), 509–528.
11. Wisensale, *Family Leave Policy*.
12. Ronald Reagan, "Radio Address to the Nation on Family Values," December 20, 1986, accessed on the American Presidency Project, http://www.presidency.ucsb.edu/ws/index.php?pid=36826.
13. Joyce Lynn, "Washington Day Care,"*Early Childhood Education Journal* 3 (1976).
14. Phyllis Schlafly, "Time to Defund Feminist Pork," *Eagle Forum Column*, July 20, 2005.
15. Wisensale, *Family Leave Policy*.

Index

abortion
  availability of, 76–82
  "family values" policies and, 182
  fertility paradox and, 169–170
  poverty and, 87–90
Advocate Health and Hospitals Corporation, 55
Affordable Health Care Options (AHCO), 152–153
After-School Alliance, 135–136
AHIC programs, 96–97
Alabama, 81
Alan Guttmacher Institute, 79
American Academy of Pediatrics, 109
American Association for Labor Legislation, 174
American Express, 65–66
American Prospect (Hirshman), 26
Ameriplan, 149, 152–153
A-Plus Early Learning Center, 131, 193
Argentina, 100–101
at-home infant care (AHIC) programs, 96–97, 114–120, 191–192
attachment theory, 117
Australia, 101
Austria, 100
Avon, 144
Belgium, 166, 167
Belkin, Lisa, 24–25, 61
Belsky, Jay, 127–128
Bennetts, Leslie, 57–60
Bernstein, Jared, 49
Better Business Bureau, 153
Bianchi, Suzanne, 50
Biden, Joe, 194
Bimbo Bakeries, 27–28
birth control
  fertility paradox and, 169–170
  poverty and, 79, 83, 91
  See also reproductive choice
birth rate. *See* fertility paradox
blame, 21
  blaming attitude toward mothers, 27–29
  "family values" policies and, 180–187
  gender equity and, 177–179
  government-issued family support *vs.*, 172–173
  historical maternity leave proposals and, 173–177, 179–180, 185–186
Bolivia, 100
bonding, 117. *See also* family leave
Bowlby, John, 117
Brazelton, T. Berry, 117
breast-feeding, 64, 108–110

Buchanan, Pat, 137
Bureau of Labor Statistics, 39
Bush, George W., 19, 122, 182
Busy Bees Preschool, 192

CafeMom.com, 143
Caferro, Mary, 113
California, 148, 185–186
Carter, Jimmy, 180
Center for American Progress, 136
Center for Law and Social Policy, 72, 122
Center for Women and Work, 184
Center for Work-Life Policy, 66
child care, 26, 121–126, 136–140, 157–158
  at-home infant care (AHIC) programs, 191–192
  debt incurred from, 123, 126, 136
  doulas and, 172–173
  "family values" policies and, 181, 182
  fertility paradox and, 163, 166
  income level and, 63, 68
  for preschoolers and school-age children, 132–136
  quality of, 126–132
  support systems and, 44
  time spent on, by working mothers, 49–50
  See also public policy (U.S.)
Child Care Services Bureau (New York State), 119
Child Trends, 112
Chile, 101
choice. *See* abortion; fertility paradox
Citibank, 123
Clinton, Bill, 82, 98, 113, 183
Clinton, Hillary, 118
Comprehensive Child Care Development Act, 137
Consolidated Catfish, 74, 86
contraception. *See* birth control
Cotter, David, 15–19, 170
courtship, division of household chores and, 47
Creating a Life (Hewlett), 91
Crist, Charlie, 138
Crittenden, Ann, 58, 85
Crunch: Why Do I Feel So Squeezed? (Bernstein), 49
Czech Republic, 101

De Bruin, Ellen, 155
DeGroot, Jessica, 53–54
Denmark, 138, 165
Department of Human Services (Mississippi), 82
depression
  emotional support of mothers and, 44
  family leave and, 111–112
  fertility paradox and, 167–169
  See also mental health issues
Direct Selling Association, 146
Discovery Me Preschool, 129–130
divorce, division of household chores and, 51
domestic chores. *See* household chores
doulas, 172–173
Dow Jones, 110
Durst, Christine, 144–146, 147–148, 149
Dutch Women Don't Get Depressed (de Bruin), 155

Eberhard-Gran, Malin, 111
economy, 15–19
  gender equity and, 15–19
  of Hollandale, Mississippi, 73–75, 86–87
  recession and income gap among working mothers, 70–73
  See also income; poverty
education
  child-care advantages and, 128, 133–134
  poverty and, 86–90
employment, 167
  blaming attitude toward mothers, 27–29
  division of household chores and time spent at work, 52–53
  "family-friendly" companies, 98–99
  fertility paradox and, 167–169
  full-time *vs.* part-time statistics, 149–150
  gender equity and, 15–19, 170–171, 177–179
  "opting out" of, 24–27, 61–62, 66, 67–70
  overwork and, 42
  women in workforce (statistics), 182
  World War II and, 179
  See also child care; family leave; public policy (U.S.); reproductive choice; *individual names of countries*
"End of the U.S. Gender Revolution, The" (Cotter), 18–19
Equally Shared Parenting, 53, 56
Equal Pay Act, 17–18
Ernst & Young, 66
European Union
  fertility paradox and, 165–166
  on part-time work, 153
  See also individual names of countries
exercise, 40

Families and Work Institute, 42, 99
Family and Medical Leave Act, 19, 96–97, 98, 102, 105, 116, 183
family leave, 1–2, 12–13, 35–36, 93–97, 193–194
  at-home infant care (AHIC) programs, 96–97, 114–120
  breast-feeding and, 108–110
  Family and Medical Leave Act, 96–97, 98, 102, 105, 116, 183
  fertility paradox and, 166
  historical maternity leave proposals and, 173–177
  international policies on, 99–101, 110–111
  mental health issues and, 111–112
  part-time/flexible work schedules and, 105–108, 141
  "plunge" models of, 107, 120
  U.S. policy and, 97–99, 102–105, 112–113
Family Support Act, 113
"family values" policies, 78, 180–187. *See also* blame; reproductive choice
Federal Trade Commission (FTC), 147–148
Feminine Mistake: Are We Giving Up Too Much?, The (Bennetts), 57–60
Feminine Mystique, The (Friedan), 58
feminism, gender equity and, 177–179
Fertility and Sterility, 92
fertility paradox, 160–162
  defined, 165
  international approaches and, 160–168, 170–171
  mental health issues and, 167–169
  "replacement level" and, 161
  U.S. fertility rates and, 169–170
  U.S. gender equity and, 171
  U.S. public policy and, 162–167
Finland
  family leave, 101
  fertility, 165, 167
flexible work schedules. *See* part-time work
Florida, 121–122, 129–132, 138
Folbre, Nancy, 23
food security, 83
France
  doulas and, 172–173
  family leave and, 100
  fertility paradox and, 166, 167
  maternity leave policy of, 174
FreelanceHomeWriters.com, 144
freelance workforce, 68
Friedan, Betty, 58
Friedman, Don, 119
gays, division of household chores and, 50
gender equity, 15–19, 170–171, 177–179
gender roles. *See* household chores
Germany
  family/maternity leave and, 100, 174
  part-time work and, 153
Global Institute on Working Families, 100
Gornick, Janet, 138
Greenberg, Mark, 136

happiness, measuring, 156, 162. *See also* mental health issues
Happiness Studies, 156
Hastings Center for WorkLife Law, 55–56
health care/health insurance, 9–10
  freelance workforce and, 68
  part-time work and, 150–153
  pregnancy and, 174
  reproductive choice and poverty, 76–82, 87–90
Hermsen, Joan, 15–19
heterosexual couples, division of household chores and, 50
Hewlett, Sylvia Ann, 65, 71, 91
Heymann, Jody, 63, 100
high-profile professionals, 57–60, 73–75
  alternative work schedules for, 65–67
  childlessness and, 90–92
  effect of recession on, 70–73
  fantasy problems of, 60–62
  flexible work schedules and, 105–108
  income gap between high- and low-income workers, 62–65
  work as optional and, 61–62, 66, 67–70
  See also income
Hirshman, Linda, 26
Hitler, Adolf, 164
Hochschild, Arlie, 41
Hollandale, Mississippi, 73–75, 86–87
Hong Kong, 160
household chores, 37–40
  changing roles of men and, 49, 54–56
  expectations and, 47–51
  finding balance and, 52–54
  policy and, 44, 47
  tag-team parenting and, 51–52
  time spent on, 40–47
housing, poverty and, 83

I Don't Know How She Does It (Pearson), 59–60
income
  child care and, 63
  childless women and, 90–92

income (*continued*)
financial impact of motherhood on, 84–87
gender gap and, 17–19, 67
income gap between high- and low-income workers, 62–65
of partners and division of household chores, 50–51
part-time work and, 149–150, 153
See also economy; high-profile professionals; poverty
infertility, 7–8. *See also* fertility paradox
Institute for Health and Social Policy, McGill University, 100
Institute for Women's Policy Research, 90, 99
International Labor Organization (ILO), 173–174
Internet, multilevel-marketing schemes and, 143–147
"I Pay Childcare" (Citibank), 123, 126
Irma Hunter Wesley Child Development Center, 139
Islam, 111
"Is the Fetus a Person?" (Schroedel), 83
Italy, 161, 164

Jackson Women's Health Organization, 76, 80, 81
Japan, 168
Journal of Family Issues, 42

Killing the Black Body (Roberts), 176
Kilpatrick, James, 181
Knussman, Howard Kevin, 29, 55

Lathrop, Julia, 175
Latin American culture, family leave and, 111
Latinos, fertility and, 170
Ledbetter, Lilly, 19
Lehman Bros., 71
lesbians, division of household chores and, 50
Lopez, Yaire, 27–28
Lopoo, Leonard M., 87
Loubet, Susan, 115–116
Loubet, Thom, 116
Lucero, Loretta, 119
Lust, Jerry, 29
Lust, Tracy, 28–29

Macau, 160
Madden, Elizabeth, 108
Melaleuca, 142–143, 146–147
Mary Kay, 146, 147
Maternity and Infancy Act of 1921, 177
maternity leave. *See* family leave
McCain, John, 30
McDonald, Peter, 165
McGee, Cheryl, 81
McGill University, 100
Medicaid, 151–152
men
changing roles of, and household chores, 49, 54–56
child-care responsibilities and employment, 29
"daddy leave" in Sweden, 166
income of, and division of household chores, 50–51
See also family leave; household chores
mental health issues
emotional support of mothers and, 44
family leave policy and, 111–112
fertility paradox and, 167–169
happiness and, 156, 162
Minnesota, 118
Mississippi
abortion availability in, 76–82
child poverty in, 77
economy of Hollandale, 73–75, 86–87
fertility paradox and, 169–170
"mommy wars," 25
Montana, 113–114, 117, 118, 147
Moore, Michael, 172–173
Moral Majority, 181
motherhood
blaming attitude toward mothers, 27–29
as "choice," 23–24
financial costs of, 84–87
"opting out" of workforce for, 24–27, 61–62, 66, 67–70
"Supermom" myth of, 29–36
See also fertility paradox; poverty; reproductive choice
"motherhood experiment." *See* fertility paradox
"mothering" care, 117
Ms., 116
multilevel-marketing schemes, 142–143
in foreign countries, 154
FTC investigations of, 147–148
women targeted by, 143–147
Mulvihill, Jemilla, 150–152
Mussolini, Benito, 164

National Bureau of Economic Research, 111

National Campaign to Prevent Teen and Unplanned Pregnancy, 91
National Computer Systems Company, 28
National Federation of Business and Professional Women, 178–179
National Institute of Child Health and Human Development, 129
National Partnership for Women & Families, 175
National Sleep Foundation, 32
National Woman's Party, 178–179
National Women's Law Center, 90
Netherlands
  fertility paradox and, 162, 167, 170
  part-time work and, 154–159
Network Marketing Game, The (Taylor), 146
New Jersey, 184–186
New Mexico, 96–97, 113, 114–116, 118, 119–120
New Mexico Women's Agenda, 115
New York (state), 119, 133–134
New York Times Magazine, 24, 53, 61
Nigeria, 111
"Nine Point Family Plan" (Carter), 180
Nixon, Richard, 137
Norway
  family leave, 100
  fertility, 163, 165
nursing, 64, 108–110

Obama, Barack, 136, 194–195
Off Ramps and On Ramps (Hewlett), 65
Opting Out? Why Women Really Quit Careers and Head Home (Stone), 61–62
"'Opt Out' or Pushed Out?" (Williams), 25
"Opt-Out Revolution, The" (*New York Times Magazine*), 24, 61

Palin, Sarah, 30–32, 62
part-time work, 105–108, 141–142
  "family values" policies and, 182
  fertility paradox and, 163
  health insurance and, 150–153
  income level and, 65–67
  international approaches to, 153–159
  multilevel-marketing schemes and, 142–150
  public policy and, 176
paternity leave. *See* family leave; men
Pearson, Allison, 59–60
pensions, 176
Perfect Madness: Motherhood in the Age of Anxiety (Warner), 58, 61
Peter Pan Child Development Center, 130
Pew Research Center, 38, 149
"pink collar" jobs, 17–19
PinkTruth.org, 147
poverty
  birth of babies and, 13–15
  child care and, 63, 192–193
  childless women and, 90–92
  family leave and, 99
  financial costs of motherhood and, 84–87
  income gap among working mothers and, 70–75
  public policy and, 82–84
  reproductive choice and, 76–82, 87–90
  See also income
pregnancy
  health care coverage and, 151–152, 174
  reproductive choice and, 76–82, 87–90 (*See also* poverty)
Pregnancy Insurance, 152
pre-kindergarten programs, 133–134
premature birth, 9–13
preschoolers, child care and, 132–136
Presser, Harriet, 51
Price of Motherhood, The (Crittenden), 58, 85
"pro-choice"/"pro-life." *See* abortion
Pro-Life Mississippi, 79
pronatalist policies. *See* fertility paradox
public policy (U.S.), 4, 21–22
  child care and, 121–126, 136–140
  "family values" policies and, 180–187
  fertility paradox and, 162–167
  gender equity and, 15–19, 170–171, 177–179
  government-issued family support *vs.*, 172–173
  historical maternity leave proposals and, 173–177, 179–180, 185–186
  household chores and time issues, 44, 47
  Obama administration on, 136, 194–195
  poverty and, 82–84
  women in government, 17, 167
Pyramid Scheme Alert, 146
pyramid schemes. *See* multilevel-marketing schemes

Reagan, Ronald, 82, 180–183, 186–187
recession. *See* economy
religion
  Catholicism and fertility paradox, 164–165
  cultural views on maternity leave and, 111
  "family values" policies and, 180

reproductive choice
"family values" policies and, 182
fertility paradox and, 169–170
poverty and, 76–82, 87–90
See also fertility paradox
Roberts, Dorothy, 176
Rockefeller Foundation, 175

Salon.com, 73
same-sex couples, division of household chores and, 50
Sanchez, Linda Carmona, 131, 193
Schlafly, Phyllis, 26, 137
school-age children, child care and, 132–136
Schroedel, Jean Reith, 83
second shift, 41
sex education, 83
Sex Roles, 84
sexuality, time issues and, 43
Sicko (Moore), 172–173
Simon, Robin, 168
Singapore, 164
single motherhood, 83–84
fertility paradox and, 170
National Campaign to Prevent Teen and Unplanned Pregnancy, 91
See also poverty; public policy (U.S.)
sleep, 40
social-benefit systems, fertility and, 161
Social Security Act, 176
Spain, 100
special needs children, 9–13, 68–70, 188–191
Staffcentrix, 144–146, 147–148, 149
stay-at-home moms, multilevel-marketing schemes and, 142–150. *See also* child care; part-time work; poverty; reproductive choice
Steinem, Gloria, 116
Stone, Pamela, 61
"striking," by mothers, 46
Study of Early Child Care and Youth Development, 128
"Supermom" myth, 29–36
Sweden
child care in, 138
family leave, 100
fertility paradox and, 166–167
maternity leave policy of, 174
part-time work in, 159

tag-team parenting, 51–52
Taylor, Jon M., 146
teenage pregnancy, 91, 170. *See also* poverty; public policy (U.S.)
Temporary Assistance for Needy Families (TANF), 96, 119
Texas, 152
ThirdPath, 53–54
Thompson, Betty, 79–80
Time, 175

United Kingdom, 153
United States. *See* public policy (U.S.); *individual names of agencies*
University of Maryland–College Park, 51
U.S. Army, 112, 146
U.S. Center on Budget and Policy Priorities, 83
U.S. Department of Agriculture, 85
U.S. Department of Labor, 98, 175, 179
U.S. Supreme Court, 178

Vachon, Amy, 53–54
Vachon, Marc, 53–54, 56
Vanneman, Reeve, 15–19
Veenhoven, Ruut, 155–156

wages. *See* income
Wal-Mart, 102–104
Walsh, Shireen, 28
Warner, Judith, 58, 61
"War on Moms," 2–5
Washington, D.C., 77
Washington (state), 185–186
wealthy mothers. *See* high-profile professionals
Weissman, Myrna, 168
welfare policy
blame and, 176
family leave and, 112–113, 119
See also poverty; public policy (U.S.)
Welfare Reform Act, 82, 113
White, Karen, 184
Widener Anmarie, 158
Widening Gap, The (Heymann), 63
Williams, Joan, 25
Work-at-Home-Mothers' Web site, 144
Work Incentives Program, 112–113
Working for Equality and Economic Liberation (WEEL), 113–114
Working Mother, 99
World Database of Happiness, 156
World of Love Early Childhood Academy, 88

YTB Travel, 146, 148

"zombymoms," 20–22